THE LOGIC OF CONFORMITY

Japan's Entry into International Society

JAPAN AND GLOBAL SOCIETY

How has Japan shaped, and been shaped by, globalization – politically, economically, socially, and culturally? How has its identity, and how have its objectives, changed? *Japan and Global Society* explores Japan's past, present, and future interactions with the Asia Pacific and the world from a wide variety of disciplinary and interdisciplinary perspectives and through diverse paradigmatic lenses. Titles in this series are intended to showcase international scholarship on Japan and its regional neighbours that will appeal to scholars in disciplines both in the humanities and the social sciences.

Japan and Global Society is supported by generous grants from the Shibusawa Eiichi Memorial Foundation and the University of Missouri–St Louis.

For a list of books published in the series, see page 191.

The Logic of Conformity

Japan's Entry into International Society

TOMOKO T. OKAGAKI

UNIVERSITY OF TORONTO PRESS
Toronto Buffalo London

Toronto Buffalo London
www.utppublishing.com

ISBN 978-1-4426-4188-4

Publication cataloguing information is available from Library and Archives Canada

University of Toronto Press acknowledges the financial assistance to its publishing program of the Canada Council for the Arts and the Ontario Arts Council.

Canada Council for the Arts Conseil des Arts du Canada

ONTARIO ARTS COUNCIL
CONSEIL DES ARTS DE L'ONTARIO
50 YEARS OF ONTARIO GOVERNMENT SUPPORT OF THE ARTS
50 ANS DE SOUTIEN DU GOUVERNEMENT DE L'ONTARIO AUX ARTS

University of Toronto Press acknowledges the financial support of the Government of Canada through the Canada Book Fund for its publishing activities.

To Alyssa, Leo, Ray

Contents

Preface

The University of Toronto Press, in cooperation with the University of Missouri–St Louis, and the Shibusawa Eiichi Memorial Foundation of Tokyo, is launching an ambitious new series, "Japan and Global Society." The volumes in the series will explore how Japan has defined its identities and objectives in the larger region of Asia and the Pacific, and, at the same time, how the global community has been shaped by Japan and its interactions with other countries.

The dual focus on Japan and on global society reflects the series editors' and publishers' commitment to globalizing national studies. Scholars and readers have become increasingly aware that it makes little sense to treat a country in isolation. All countries are interdependent and shaped by cross-national forces so that mono-national studies, those that examine a country's past and present in isolation, are never satisfactory. Such awareness has grown during the last few decades when global, transnational phenomena and forces have gained prominence. In the age of globalization, no country retains complete autonomy or freedom of action. Nations do continue to exist, and they act in pursuit of their respective national interests, which frequently results in international tensions. Financial, social, and educational policies continue to be defined domestically, with national communities as units. But transnational economic, environmental, and cultural forces always infringe upon national entities, transforming them in subtle and sometimes even violent ways. Global society, consisting of billions of individuals and their organizations, evolves and shapes national communities even as the latter contributes to defining the overall human community.

Japan provides a particularly pertinent instance of such interaction, but this series is not limited to studies of that country alone. Indeed, the books published in the series will show that there is little unique about Japan, whose history has been shaped by interactions with China, Korea, the United States, and many other countries. For this reason, we shall publish volumes dealing with countries in the Asia-Pacific region and comparing their respective developments and shared destinies. At the same time, it is expected that some studies in the series will transcend national frameworks and discuss more transnational themes, such as humanitarianism, migrations, and diseases, documenting how these phenomena have impacted upon Japan and other countries and how, at the same time, they have contributed to the making of a more interdependent global society.

Lastly, it is hoped that the studies we publish will help promote an understanding of non-national entities, such as regions, religions, and civilizations. Modern history as well as current affairs continue to be examined in terms of nations as the key units of analysis, and yet these other entities have had their own vibrant histories that have not coincided with nation-centered narratives. To look at Japan, or for that matter any other country, and to examine its past and present in these alternative frameworks will enrich our understanding of modern world history and of the contemporary global civilization.

Akira Iriye

Author's Note

Japanese names in the following chapters are given in their original order with the family name preceding the first except in identifying the authors of publications in the notes. All dates have been converted to conform to the Western calendar. Any unintended errors, mistakes, or omissions of facts, translation, and spellings are my responsibility alone.

THE LOGIC OF CONFORMITY

Japan's Entry into International Society

PART ONE

The Framework of Analysis

1 Introduction: Explaining Japan's Entry into the International System

This study examines the socialisation of Japan into the European state system in the latter half of the nineteenth century as an aspect of expansion and institutionalisation of the European international system by asking the following questions: (1) What explains Japan's rapid socialisation into the European sovereign state system in the late nineteenth century? and (2) How can Japan's entry into the European state system be placed in the larger context of the European state system's institutionalisation? While sovereign statehood has permeated the entire globe to become one of the most universal features of international relations today, no complete explanation for this exists. Why has the European state system prevailed over other international systems in different subregions of the world and why has the Western sense of territorial statehood eventually become accepted as the standard form of political entity throughout the world? My ultimate concern, therefore, is how and why the Westphalian system has been maintained and institutionalised by accommodating changes brought by newcomers.

In examining these questions, I will employ the wisdom of a number of social science theories: structuralism, originally developed by European linguists and anthropologists[1] that International Relations (IR) scholars partially borrowed; the English School of International Relations, which explores the evolution of the societal aspects of international relations in history[2]; and new institutionalism, introduced by economic historians and widely applied to other social sciences,[3] to name a few. One of the important overlapping elements among these theories is the tension and interaction between the systemic/societal constraints and the choices that actors make. In this study, I will treat interstate systems as institutions that possess certain functions, rules, and norms that constrain the behaviour of actors for the stability, regulation, and preservation of the value of the existent society.[4] I will then examine Japan's response to such a systemic necessity of international relations in the nineteenth century.

The central puzzle that runs through the study is the high degree of conformity that Japan demonstrated in accommodating itself to Western norms of international relations within a short period of time. Only four decades after its first encounter with the West in 1853, it joined the Western powers in the European colonial competition in East Asia. The slogan of "expel the barbarians" (*jōi*), which prevailed during the early days of the encounter with the West, was transformed to "civilisation and enlightenment" (*bunmei kaika*) by 1880. Why did Japan join the Western state system without voicing as much resistance as other Asian countries, such as China, did? What explains Japan's rapid transformation from a feudal society to a modern nation-state? The answers to these questions may provide insights into the foreign policy behaviour of newcomers to the European state system in general and enhance our understanding of the evolution of the international norms in the particular historical context of the nineteenth century. While there are many books that describe various features of Japan's modernisation, its entry into the international system and socialisation has not been directly taken up as a political science subject, but rather has been studied as a history subject.[5] Historians' approach to the subject is characterised by voluntarism that interprets the unfolding events as introduced by human agent as the locomotive for incremental transformation and by their emphasis on questioning "how" instead of "why" certain events occurred. Explanations for Japan's rapid socialisation with Western norms in the late nineteenth century and its applicability to other cases still remain partial and largely unexamined.

My main argument in this study is that the relative rapidity of Japan's entry into the sovereign state system can be explained by the normative change in nineteenth-century international society, where Japanese leaders perceived congruity with the domestic preparedness for modernisation. As Japan faced the particular state-building *problematique* of the positivist norm of the nineteenth century, its modes of modernisation and development were defined by this prevalent norm of sovereign statehood shared by the European club of international relations. The leaders needed to comprehend the requirements for membership and find ways to mobilise and transform dormant domestic institutions into those that suited the European criteria in order to obtain full sovereign statehood.

In studying the interplay between the systemic and domestic constraints and opportunities that leaders faced, I will pay particular attention to the development of international law as an important index of how the international system was institutionalised. As is widely perceived, the nineteenth century not only experienced increased legalisation of rules that bound states in the spheres of commerce and warfare, but also underwent a paradigmatic shift in international law from natural to positive law, displacing the universal notion of equality among states based on morality to a constitutive one.[6] During this shift, a "standard of civilisation" emerged as a prevalent norm and was forced on the newcomer states.[7] The timing of Japan's entry coincides with this positivist turn in international law, which bound the way newcomers entered the family of nations.

What facilitated Japan's conformist response to the "standard of civilisation" was the availability of domestic institutions conducive to the Western style of modernisation, as well as by the leaders' maneuvring to incorporate the international norms in order to direct the country towards modernisation with the objective of obtaining membership in international society. The existence of such domestic institutions reduced the cost of conformance for Japan when the positivist turn in international law opened up an opportunity for Japan to modify its traditional domestic institutions into ones compatible with modern institutions that would accord with Western norms. During the process of socialisation between 1853 and 1899, the leaders saw expediency in abiding by international law as a means to enhance their national interests, first, as a "shield of the weak," and later, as a "tool of the strong."[8]

What I would like to achieve in this study is to provide a systemic perspective in explaining Japan's entry into the international system and to draw broader applicability to newcomers' socialisation into the international system. By examining how Japan tried to comply with the norm of statehood in international society, I will also explore the implications of Japan's socialisation for the persistence and strength of the existing international system. I hypothesise that the logic of conformity of newcomers is closely tied with the logic of persistence of the Westphalian sovereign state system.

The Intellectual Landscape: Alternative Views on Japan's Entry

I begin by conducting an overview of how previous scholars have explained Japan's entry and socialisation into international society. Generally speaking, the discourse on the topic can be categorised into two types of arguments. One emphasises the underlying unintended forces embedded in the nature of the international system that constrain actors; another emphasises attributes of actors, including domestic institutions, plus manipulations and choices that the human agents make based on interests and preferences.

The Power Configuration of the International System

The most obvious explanation for Japan's socialisation into international society is that Japan was simply "forced" to socialise. The explanation accords with the traditional view of international relations whose essence is outlined in Thucydides's felicities: "The strong do what they have the power to do and the weak accept what they must."[9] In other words, the power configuration of international relations during the nineteenth century defined Japan's course. Empowered especially after the Industrial Revolution, Europeans and Americans appeared to the Japanese as too strong to chase away. There was no chance Japan could resist the demands of the Western powers equipped with strong military and economic power, backed by rapid industrial and technological development.[10]

As the most explicit statement of international systemic imperatives imposed on actors that explains the long-term patterns of international politics with elegance and rigour,[11] neorealist theory in IR considers an actor's behaviour as moulded by structural forces, which encourages similarities in the foreign policy behaviour and outcomes of all states despite their different domestic-level attributes. States conform to common international practices even if, for internal reasons, they would prefer not to. An international system exercises a compliance pull autonomously of state interests and other attributes, narrowing the range of state behaviour. In Kenneth Waltz's theory, structural effects are manifested in two ways: first, by socialising actors, and second, by competition among actors.[12] Socialisation constrains and reforms actors' behaviour, while competition encourages actors to comply with the way most accepted and most successful. Thus, structural effects in neorealism indicate a selection mechanism that rewards certain behaviour and punishes others. The behaviour of international actors who try to survive in the system then starts to share similar characteristics, creating orderly patterns.

In the late nineteenth century, with the European-dominated international relations of the time, Asian states faced such systemic forces and, in the end, they all conformed to Western norms of international society, obtaining "membership" sooner or later. The theoretical rigour of the structural explanation in analysing long-term international phenomena, however, does not help us understand how individual actors respond to the same systemic constraints differently. As Waltz himself notes, structural effects are general and indirect. They only narrow the variety of foreign policy outcomes of actors.[13] While it provides the most general explanation for Japan's overall response to the West during this period and illustrates why Japan was obliged to accept Western demands to open the country, the structural explanation misses several important aspects of Japan's socialisation. Why, for example, was Japan not colonised as some other Asian countries were, if its weakness was so plainly exposed to the Western eyes? How can it explain Japan's subsequent rapid modernisation after being forced to open itself up? Yielding to the West would not necessarily have led to the unusual efforts that Japanese leaders made in adopting Western norms and modern state apparatus and in demonstrating their national capability to the West. The structural explanation fails to account for the conformist behaviour that followed and seemed more voluntary than forced. Other factors must have caused the positive attitudes and capacity that Japan showed in conforming to the Western norms.

Following a conventional method of examining the general systemic factors that circumscribe actors' behaviours and then domestic factors that explain what was left to be explained after the systemic analysis, my study starts by examining the basic structural forces of the nineteenth-century international system that constrained the behaviours of the international actors. The study will then turn to an examination of Japan's response to such systemic constraints in accommodating itself.[14]

Structural Arguments with Time Dimensions

Scholars of state building, industrial policy, and democratisation in comparative politics and sociology have often offered more fine-grained structural explanations by introducing a time dimension. Charles Tilly, who is well known for his study on the formation of national states in Western Europe, recognises, for example, that, while West European state building can be explained by domestic variables, the state building of latecomer states cannot be adequately explained by internal logic alone, and that external dimensions play a larger role for them.[15] Similarly, in the literature on industrialisation and modernisation, Alexander Gerschenkron and Albert Hirschman contend that the timing of industrialisation defines the speed, the domestic institutions, and the strategies required for economic development.[16] As another example, Robert Jackson's quasi-state thesis explains the survival of contemporary statehood in the third world on the basis of the institutionalised nature of the "negative sovereignty regime" that today's sovereign state system imposes on the actors.[17]

These works suggest the importance of timing in defining the way a state engages in state building, modernisation, and industrialisation. As the content and the method of state socialisation is constrained by the prevalent norms of statehood and the shared level of development of the day, it is essential to examine the time-contingent structure of the international system of the nineteenth century in explaining the entry process of Japan. As will be shown later, the international norms reflected in the positive international law developed during the nineteenth century posed constraints on the foreign policy behaviour of international actors, of which Japan became a part.

In the narrower time frame of the East Asian context, the "timing" of the arrival of the West has often been mentioned as one of the most plausible explanations for Japan's rapid socialisation into international society. Regarded as a small, poor country, located on the periphery of East Asia, Japan had been somewhat ignored by European powers at the first stage of their expansion in the region. While the vast size of China attracted the West, the marginal dimensions of Japan and its scarcity in natural resources, were not very appealing. Because of this lucky neglect, Japan's encounter with the West fell ten years behind China's, which gave Japan sufficient time to learn what was going on in other parts of Asia and to prepare for the coming encounter.[18]

This view provides important general background for some aspects of Japan's socialisation with the West. It explains, for example, why Japan was not colonised while China and India were, at least partially. Keenly aware of what was going on in other parts of Asia, Japanese leaders seriously discussed how Japan should respond to the West in order to avoid the fate of their neighbours.[19] For their part, the Western powers gradually lost their interest in colonialisation after encountering considerable rebellion and anti-European sentiment in China and India. With Japan, therefore, they tended to want just friendly commercial relations.

While this time lag factor provides another common-sense explanation, other important features of Japan's entry into the international system are not addressed. For example, even though the Japanese leaders might have been aware of the fate of China and other parts of the non-European world, how was it possible to prepare itself to avoid the same fate if the country was not stronger than the West? Moreover, although it is common to compare Japan's case with China's, comparison with other countries may invalidate this claim. The West came to Thailand later than Japan, for example, but this did not necessarily make the Thai socialisation process faster or smoother than its Japanese counterpart.[20] It took Thailand much longer than Japan to acquire complete membership in international society. Other causes that led different countries in Asia to different paths of socialisation must be identified.

The Cultural-Psychological Explanation

If the primacy of the "whole" or international system is the characteristic of the structuralist argument, the primacy of the "parts" or states as actors is that of the domestic explanation. Explanations that place emphasis on agentic attributes to account for Japan's socialisation into international society can be largely divided into two types: cultural and isomorphist.

Once popular among anthropologists as well as among political scientists, the cultural explanations try to clarify the mechanism of Japan's modernisation and adaptation to Western norms by intrinsic aspects of the country. Several traits of the Japanese culture and psyche that emphasise the uniqueness of Japan have often been pointed out here.

First, Japan's island-nation mentality, fostered by geographical factors as well as by three hundred years of isolation before the arrival of Admiral Perry, is said to have worked as a locomotive for rapid catching up with the West. According to this view, the Japanese keenly felt a sense of threat and backwardness in the face of the technological superiority of the West due to their sensitivity to outside influences. The insularity of Japan had contributed to its awareness that superior culture and technology existed externally and could be borrowed, while China's geographical location, its status in East Asian international relations, and its sense of superiority led to an attitude of disdain for what the outside world could bring to them.[21] After the ban on occidental books was lifted in 1720, Western scientific knowledge came to be known as Dutch learning (*rangaku*) and was held in high regard, rendering Japan "a head start with the Western science and technological modernisation that most Asian countries lacked."[22] The rapidity of social change in both the Meiji period (1868–1912) and after World War II has often been ascribed to Japan's openness to foreign knowledge. The tradition of looking abroad for best practices, and of the public accepting such borrowing as legitimate, is thus an important aspect of Japan's island mentality.

Second, as Fairbank, Reischauer, and Craig mention, geographical isolation from the continent also fostered a sense of independent national identity, making it relatively easy for Japan to accept a plurality of the world consisting of equal sovereign states with no dominant state claiming universal rule. "In the nineteenth century, while the Chinese found the multi-state, international system of Europe wholly unacceptable, the Japanese could quickly understand and accept it, and begin to act accordingly."[23] Japan, in other words, already possessed the basis for the concept of a nation-state that accepts the anarchical nature of international life, composed as it was of sovereign states.

Third, the ethics and morals of Japan's military culture are also often mentioned as cultural-psychological traits of the Japanese that blended well with the Western international norms. Historical documents show that Westerners living in China and Japan often identified differences in the mentalities of the Chinese and the Japanese, contrasting the proclivities of the Chinese, whose preference was to be governed by intellectuals, with those of the Japanese, who preferred to be led by soldiers. "As feudal military men Japanese leaders had a more realistic understanding of military technology than did the scholar-gentry leadership of China. Unlike China, the Japanese did not have to be humiliated in bitter defeat before they could recognise their own military inferiority."[24] The military culture, reflected in a strong sense of shame and dishonour, is also often said to have regulated and motivated Japanese conduct in its relations with the West by fostering an unusual degree of fear that the country might be laughed at by others.[25] Japanese goal-orientedness, shown by, for instance, the tradition of living simply and frugally in order to save for a long-range economic investment, is further regarded as part of the military culture that has facilitated the adoption of Western sciences, in contrast to the status-orientedness of other Asian countries.

The cultural-psychological explanation, however, suffers from nonfalsifiability and an incapacity to present cross-sectional implications.

The problem lies in the difficulty in drawing long-term theoretical insights from the cultural-psychological traits of a nation.

Isomorphism[26]

Some scholarship has moved from the traditional East–West divide, or Asian-European distinction, towards a more objective perspective to place Japan and its modernisation in the world and in history. Two such views offered by Japanese scholars have attracted considerable attention both inside and outside Japan as interpretations of Japanese history and modernisation in larger perspectives. The two views both indicate that premodern Japan already possessed features comparable to Western Europe that were conducive to modernisation.

"AN ECOLOGICAL VIEW" OF JAPANESE HISTORY

In 1957 Umesao Tadao published a provocative essay called *An Ecological View of History*.[27] While the traditional view of Japan's modernisation was based on predominant Western concepts of history, Umesao provided a unique, refreshing view on Japan's identity and on Asia more generally. In fact, his ecological view is a model of world history rather than a model focused exclusively on Japan. Umesao identified some fundamental differences that exist between the coastal and inland areas of the Eurasian continent. According to Umesao, coastal regions, whether in the East or the West, display striking similarities when compared with inland regions, where the history is typified by the repeated emergence of strong authoritarian regimes. Coastal regions, Japanese and Western European, on the other hand, are characterised by unilinear, step-by-step development of history from feudal to modern, and increased trade and liberty.[28]

Umesao claims that dividing up the world into East and West and conceptualising the world in East–West terms ignores the region that lies in between: the vast area from Pakistan to North Africa on the Eurasian continent. According to Umesao, the differences in the social structure between the coastal and inland areas caused differences in their lifestyles and history. In Western Europe, he sees a parallel of what Japan achieved as a civilised country: industrial power, an enmeshed transportation system, an administrative system, a high level of education with a well-developed educational system, material abundance, a high standard of living, a long life expectancy, low death rate, advanced culture, art, and academics.[29] It was by irreversible historical law and consequence that Japan and Western Europe became civilised powers sharing similar conditions: temperate climate and an appropriate amount of rain, bringing high productivity. Social phenomena in coastal regions that occurred in parallel with historical steps were feudalism,[30] emergence of a citizenry, formation of guilds, development of liberal cities, international trade, farmers' rebellions, imperialist competitions, development of capitalism, and so on.[31]

Umesao's theoretical model is adopted from that of ecological succession. Succession occurs due to the accumulated interactions between actors and the environment, eventually spilling out of the framework of former lifestyles. One important point that he makes is that the step-by-step succession in the coastal area is "autogenic" with energy for development emerging from the inside of the community, while the history in the inland area is "allogenic," developed by the outside forces.[32]

"RETHINKING JAPANESE HISTORY"

Revisionist Japanese historians contend that Japan's modernisation started during the fifteenth century, when Japan underwent tremendous changes in political and social structures, not in 1853, as had commonly been thought. This school argues that, by the time Perry arrived in 1853, Japan was replete with social organisations desirous of Westernisation. One of the contentions of this school, for example, is that "feudalism" in Japan, which is supposed to have lasted until the modernisation in the nineteenth century, was quite different from the Western conceptual equivalent. "Farmers," literally translated as "one hundred surnames" (*hyakushō*) in Japanese, for example, were frequently engaged in other types of economic activities than farming,[33] which undermines the conventional wisdom that premodern Japan was essentially an agrarian society. These characteristics of the Japanese farmers are also noted by Fairbanks, Reischauer, and Craig:

> Japanese farmers were gradually becoming the most efficient producers in the world. Farming became increasingly commercialized... The great economic development of the Tokugawa period made economic modernization easier. Rich Japanese peasants, instead of investing in more land, the only relatively safe investment in most of Asia, put their wealth into trade and industry, which brought larger profits.[34]

While Umesao's *An Ecological View of History* explains Japan's modernisation by environmental attributes that Japan shared with Western Europe, revisionist Japanese historians take into consideration the importance of the existence of domestic institutions prior to the time of entry that facilitated the socialisation process, such as postal service, educational institutions, monetary economy, availability of printed materials, and the bureaucratic tradition experienced within the ruling class of the domain system that further blended well with what was required for modern government.[35] Vertical ties of loyalty that had bound feudal Japan are also said to have encouraged the hierarchical, centralised political propensity of Japan, which was congenial to modern state building.[36]

Providing fertile ground for future scholarship to explore, isomorphism promises one of the powerful explanations for the seemingly smooth process of Japan's modernisation and socialisation. On the other hand, these isomorphic features "facilitated but did not precipitate" Japanese modernisation.[37] The isomorphic elements needed to be vectored towards modernisation and compliance with international norms in order for Japan to obtain membership in international society. As the constitutive sense of sovereign statehood developed in nineteenth-century international law was now imposed on the newcomers, it needs to be explained how Japan's isomorphic features were translated into something externally acceptable. The existence of domestic institutions conducive to modernisation, the fact that Japan already had infrastructure for modernisation, therefore, was a necessary condition, but not a sufficient one, for its socialisation with Western norms.

The explanations offered by each of the previously mentioned studies based on isomorphic features, therefore, remain partial, indirectly touching on Japan's socialisation while international constraints are rarely taken into account. The inadequacy of these explanations leads us to incorporate two other types of dynamism entailed in Japan's socialisation: the systemic pressure from international society and the leaders' manipulation in vectoring the domestic institutions towards something that would suit international demand.

The Features of the Study

My goal in this study is to examine the interactions between the structural constraints of the international system and the actors' choices represented in Japan's socialisation into international society by combining the strengths of theories of IR and comparative politics and by taking into account the time and space dimensions of the international norms and social environments. Few studies that have focused on Japan's socialisation with the European state system have integrated both international systemic constraints and state-level variables. Also, while many studies have been conducted on modern state building of non-Western countries, few have systematically analysed the process of entry into the sovereign state system from a political science perspective. Further, in contrast to the large number of accumulated works on the concept of sovereignty and nation building of the states in Western Europe and the rising scholarship on quasi-states and failed states, many of which achieved their independent statehood through decolonisation, the nature of statehood and state building of Asian countries, periodically falling in between these two models, has not been fully explored.

This study claims to contribute to academia with regard to the following points. First, by treating the state system as an institution embodied in international law, it will provide a perspective to understand how certain domestic decisions are made that is thus far absent in the historical interpretation of Japan's modernisation. IR theories that emphasise the agentic roles in creating institutions have often relied on exogenous factors such as international economic interdependence, advancements in war technology, or international military competitions in accounting for the emergence of institutions.[38] External factors, in other words, have been implicitly recognised, but have been treated in an unsystematic manner. By explicitly analysing the international constraints of the positivist turn of international law in the nineteenth century, this study juxtaposes the domestic response more in perspective and offers a comprehensive, objective explanation for it.

Second, the study sheds light on a rather neglected area of the state-building literature, that is, the survival or maintenance of the state system. While explanations abound on the origin of the state in Western Europe,[39] how the system has evolved and been institutionalised since its creation is still an inadequately investigated area of the study. The factors that explain the origin of states and the state system may not necessarily be useful in explaining the survival of the system. This study, thus, has a broader goal of contributing to a better understanding of the evolution of the sovereign state as a form of universal political organisation. States survived; so did the state-system of European origin. Why did it supersede other forms of state systems, the state system of East Asia, for example? By highlighting the rationale for the persistence of the European state system, the study will also partially present a skeptical view of the "global village" argument. While the roles and functions of states continue to be transformed and reinterpreted in the era of globalisation, rendering the world an intimately connected community, the significance of sovereign statehood has not diminished as the most fundamental way to organise the world politically.[40] Despite its failure to ensure perfect peace and justice among countries, it has proven to provide minimum order, to limit conflict, and to sustain conditions where international communication and cooperation could grow. As an institutionalised system, it plays a conservative role in accommodating new changes, giving conformist incentives to its members.

Third, this study aims at providing a political scientist's explanation for Japan's modernisation and entry into the international system, while bridging political science, international law, and history. The importance of dialogue between scholars of political science and history has often been noted, especially in academic circles where IR scholarship traditionally based itself on historical studies.[41] Recent IR scholarship in the US has increasingly demonstrated a tendency to emphasise the importance of crossing disciplinary lines between international law and international politics, too.[42] The feasibility of crossfertilisation among these disciplines is significant in analysing Japan's entry into international society.

It goes without saying that a caveat on the possible interdisciplinary tensions among them also needs to be heeded.[43] It is a common understanding, for example, that historians tend to regard history as a process, which renders description of events rather thick as an objective itself, while political scientists tend to "use" history in order to prove their theories.[44] As a disciple of political science, a field more committed to generalisation than history is, I seek universal patterns in explaining Japan's case that are applicable to the entry of the other Asian countries into the international system in general, of the latecomer's entrance in general, and then of state socialisation in general. In the course of drawing generalisations, I respect historians' attitudes of pursuing truth through an extensive excavation of historical materials and prudence in interpreting them, and try to base my arguments on firm facts. In claiming a political scientist generalisation, I also argue against the tendency of studies on Japan laden with an emphasis on its uniqueness and intrinsic traits represented, for example, by the "normalcy" debate that has occupied much space in discussions on Japanese foreign policy behaviour for the past couple of decades.[45] One of my objectives here is to demystify the tenacious exoticism and subjectivism still prevalent in Japanology. Placed in perspective, Japan's foreign policy behaviour is nothing abnormal. It affords a general social science explanation.

Ideally, the theoretical claims here should be tested against a number of case studies in order to draw generalisations from the case of Japan. In expecting critiques against the single-case nature of this study, I try to maintain a cross-sectional comparative perspective in analysing the case of Japan and refer to other Asian countries as much as possible. I also have in mind longitudinal comparative case studies. Parallel theoretical claims can be made, for example, in explaining Japan's foreign policy behaviour during its state building era after the Battle of Hakusukinoe in the seventh century as well as in the post–World War II era of restoring sovereign statehood after defeat and devastation. By basing the study on the achievements made by the community of scholars, especially the observations made by scholars of state building and nation building, I hope to contribute to a large trove of scholarly literature. This work, therefore, will not exist in isolation from the accumulated knowledge of others. As investigation of the theme involves multiple variables of nuanced weight and complexity, I believe that even a study on a single instance could illuminate the important process in a holistic way.[46]

* * *

The study consists of three parts. The first part offers theoretical perspectives to the study. Chapter 2 focuses on the two key concepts: "state socialisation" and "institutionalisation." I will start by discussing some theories of IR and comparative politics that touch on the concept of "state socialisation." While "state socialisation" is a fairly new concept, most of the existing theories in fact refer to it in one way or another, since it entails the agent-structure problem,[47] an eternal theme of many subjects in social science. As in "state socialisation," the concept of "institutionalisation" involves tensions and interactions between agents and structures. I will start with a discussion of the concept of institutions and move on to discuss institutionalisation, where I identify "autonomy" and "adaptability" as two key criteria useful in analysing the institutional persistence and dynamics of the European international system. Nineteenth-century international society, which acquired its autonomy as a Eurocentric, positivist system, also obtained complexity and adaptability as an institution during the process of accommodating the entry of Asian countries.

The second part consists of three chapters that trace the process of Japan's conformity to international law, which eventually led to the abrogation of unequal treaties concluded with the West at the early stage of their encounters. Chapter 3 examines the period of Japan's encounter with the West between 1853 and 1870. During this period of perplexity and confusion about how to engage in relations with the powerful West, the law of nations was introduced to Japan for the first time. The moderate nature of Japan's encounter with the West when compared with other non-European countries, Japan's physical preparedness for modernisation, and the existence of national leaders who identified the situation of Japan placed in the power map of world politics all contributed to a relatively accurate understanding of Western international law and to directing Japan's course of compliance with Western norms. Chapter 4 moves on to the 1870s from the earlier chaotic period, when Japan's foreign policy goal became clearly set by the political leaders as their understanding and internalisation of international law deepened, especially after the Iwakura Mission was dispatched to the United States and European countries with the objective of "absorbing" what could be applied to Japan from them. This was the era of so-called "civilisation and enlightenment," when Japan, infatuated with the West, started to adopt various institutions of a civilised state based mostly on the Prussian model and decided to "get out of Asia" (*datsua*). As admiration and adoration for the "civilised" West culminated during this period, Japan was led to accelerated modernisation and Westernisation and vigourously tried to apply the international law that it had just learned in dealing with other Asian countries, thereby demonstrating Japan's faithfulness to the Western norm. Chapter 5 turns to the final stage of negotiating the abrogation of extraterritoriality with the West, when the political leaders became increasingly aware of the reality of international law and started to demonstrate more realism and skill in adapting it for the enhancement of Japan's national interests. The Japanese leaders used international pressure to convince the domestic public, while exploiting domestic pressure to persuade the Western powers to nullify the unequal treaties. They also made various efforts to convince the West of Japan's loyalty to international law and membership in international society, basing its rationale on its lawful conduct of war during the Sino-Japanese War. The extraterritoriality finally ended in 1899, bringing Japan a diplomatic honour as the first non-European power to be fully admitted to international society. International law, which had been gradually digested and embraced since its adoption by the Japanese, became an international norm that the leaders could now manipulate to improve Japan's international status.

The third part is devoted to an analysis of the historical research and concludes the study. Several conventional views on Japan's modernisation will be questioned and refuted on the basis of the empirical evidence, where some implications for a future study of state socialisation and state building in general are drawn. The third part also places Japan's socialisation in perspective, discussing the meaning of Japan's entry for Japan itself and for international society in the larger map of institutional change in the international system.

By way of clarifying some key terms, "international law," generally conceived as consisting of international customs and treaties, refers to different manifestations in this study. It first means treatises and their content of general law of nations systematically written by international lawyers since Grotius. In Chapter 3, I mainly use the term "international law" in this sense, discussing how Japan as a novice to the rules of international society came to accept the general texts of the law of nations in the nineteenth century in search of principles that govern relations among countries. International law is also informed by intangible norms or shared ideas among countries in international society, reflecting positivism, a "standard of civilisation" based on Western customs and ideas, the notion of "might is right," and imperialism, for example. Although no inherent righteousness or value is attached to these norms, Japan embraced the spirit as a reality of the era that comprised part of the structure of international society. The Japanese political leaders who visited the United States and Europe in the special delegation in the early 1870s that I discuss in Chapter 4 picked up the essence of these norms enshrined in the spirit of Western civilisation, nurturing a strong sense of determination to modernise the country. International law further exhibits itself in concrete treaties, including unequal treaties on judicial and tax autonomy imposed on the newcomer states. As Japan's understanding of international law matured, the country started to actively engage itself in the practice of international law even in the form of correcting unjust treaties.[48]

"Entry" into an international system is considered a process rather than a particular point in history. Japan's entry in this study covers the period from its rise from subordinate, second-class status under unequal treaties with the West to the acceptance of abrogation of extraterritoriality by the West in 1899. During the process of its adjustment in conforming to the norms of the international system, it developed certain attitudes, beliefs, perceptions, and value standards regarding various functions, principles, and rules, as well as the recurrent pattern of the system itself. Although it is debatable when the entry process actually ended, I regard the acceptance of abrogation of extraterritoriality by the West as a landmark of formal recognition of Japan as an independent sovereign state by international society, which constitutes a key criterion of the Western sense of sovereign statehood based on territorial demarcation and mutual recognition.[49] From a broader perspective, therefore, Japan's entry into the sovereign state system evolved into process with further institutionalisation of the European system. Japan in turn strengthened the durability and the autonomy of the existing international system as an institution.

2 State Socialisation and Institutionalisation of the International System

This chapter clarifies two key concepts that underlie the central theoretical claims of this study: "state socialisation," which has often been implicitly discussed in many theories of international relations and comparative politics, but not explicitly studied as an independent subject in detail until recently and "institutionalisation of the international system," which constitutes a simultaneous process with state socialisation and provides insights into the rationale of the persistence of the European sovereign state system to which all countries strove to conform to in the end. The concept of institutionalisation has been forgotten since Samuel Huntington's 1968 *Political Order in Changing Societies,*[1] but it helps us analyse the sovereign state system as an institution that historically evolved by incorporating newcomer states. Both "socialisation" and "institutionalisation" are system-maintainer concepts that priviledge continuity over change. They also entail interacting processes between states as agents and the international system as a structure, being useful not only in examining how a country adjusts itself in becoming a member of international society, but also in analysing how an international system encourages a country to conform to its norms.

Theories of State Socialisation

Socialisation is generally defined as "the process by which people learn to adopt the norms, values, attitudes, and behaviours accepted and practised by the ongoing system."[2] Any discussion on socialisation presupposes that first, socialisation involves newcomers, whether they are children, trainees, novices, or infants who "become incorporated into organised patterns of interactions"; and second, socialisation involves a certain learning process where the newcomers come to adopt socially accepted "ways of thinking, feeling, and acting."[3] In other words, socialisation assumes a certain degree of hierarchy in the relations between newcomers and the authority that makes them accommodate themselves to the existing order.

Socialisation has attracted the attention of IR scholars as a concept that describes and explains compliant behaviours of states. Although treating such abstract entities as states as acting units may contradict one's common understanding of units of analysis as personal and individual, it is in the name of the state in which treaties are concluded, wars are waged, and many other types of international interactions take place. It is, therefore, justifiable to treat states as unitary political frameworks in the study of state socialisation.[4]

In the treatment of states as unitary actors, their leaders' autonomy in directing the course of state socialisation is also assumed. G. John Ikenberry and Charles A. Kupchan examine state socialisation in a hegemonic international environment and define socialisation as "a process of learning in which norms and ideals are transmitted from one party to another," emphasising the role of elites in socialisation. They note that socialisation is "the process through which national leaders internalise the norms and value orientations espoused by the hegemon and as a consequence become socialised into the community formed by the hegemon and other nations accepting its leadership position."[5] In this process, national leaders stand in between the external and the internal environment and play both international and domestic games simultaneously.[6] Leaders' successful coping with the two-level games, therefore, becomes crucial in the process of state socialisation. During the early process of Westernisation that this study focuses on, Japanese political leaders enjoyed a high degree of autonomy in managing internal and foreign affairs, relatively insulated from domestic power struggles at least until the Diet came into existence in 1890.

Structure vs. Agent: "Why" Do States Socialise?

Since how states interact with other countries and adjust themselves to the external environment constitutes one of the core themes of international politics, major IR theories all touch on state socialisation in one way or another. Two central questions regarding state socialisation are why and how countries socialise. These themes overlap those of the literature on compliance, norm diffusion, emulation, and learning.[7]

IR in Great Britain has had a long tradition of highlighting the societal aspects of international relations and their evolution where a common set of moral or legal rules binds states in their relations with one another and in the working of common institutions, forming a society.[8] Hedley Bull, representing the English School, outlines the sources of a country's socialisation with international law on two grounds: habit or inertia and deliberation or calculation of actors. In the latter, three kinds of motivations for states to obey international law are identified. First states obey laws when the law is thought to be valuable, mandatory, or obligatory, apart from its being legally required (international law of community). Second, obedience results from coercion or the threat of it by some superior power enforcing the agreement (international law of power). Third incentives to comply with international law could result from the states' interest in expecting reciprocal action by other states (international law of reciprocity), which are exemplified in mutual respect for sovereignty and the laws of war, the most central principles of international law.[9] On this point, Bull clearly states that "the importance of international law does not rest on the willingness of states to abide by its principles to the detriment of their interests, but in the fact that they so often judge it in their interests to conform to it."[10] Bull's emphasis on actors' expediency is similar to the arguments made by US institutionalists.

The neoliberal institutionalist literature in the United States treats the interests of states or individuals as a moving force of international relations. As a rational choice approach, it considers institutions as direct reflections of the voluntarist will and conscious choice of the self-interested actors, who comply and socialise with the institutions by perceiving the reduction in the transaction cost and in the information-provision mechanisms entailed in them. It is the actors' self-interest and cost-benefit calculation that leads to the creation of institutions with "persistent and connected sets of rules."[11] Once the institution is created, it exercises compliance pull by continuing to provide transaction-cost reduction and information-provision mechanisms. In institutionalist theory, therefore, the institutions switch from dependent to independent variables that "prescribe behavioral roles, constrain activity, and shape expectations."[12]

State socialisation has not formed a major theme of classical realists in IR. They have traditionally regarded states' conformity to international rules and norms as a reflection of prevailing power relations. For classical realists, national power and interests are the main driving forces that exert influence on states' behaviour. States are forced rather than encouraged to socialise themselves, if socialised at all. One variant of such realist views was hegemonic stability theory in international political economy, which explained the creation and maintenance of international regimes by relating the existence of a dominant power to stability and openness of the international economic system and cooperation among states.[13]

For neorealists, socialisation is one of the two ways the structure of the international system affects the behaviour of actors. Socialisation is a process that "reduces variety" of actors' behaviour and "encourages similarities."[14] Competition, another process of systemic influence, has similar functions. It "spurs the actors to accommodate their ways to the socially most acceptable and successful practices."[15] In this system-dominant view, order and stability are something that spontaneously and informally emerge as actors are socialised to conform to certain behavioural norms, not something contrived by voluntarist will of actors.[16]

Socialisation is also a central concept for social constructivists in IR. They focus on "logic of appropriateness" in explaining norm diffusion, where one can observe conceptual overlap with Bull's "international law of community" or international law of reciprocity as opposed to "logic of consequences." Socialisation for them is the process where intersubjective meanings of the societal norms become taken for granted.[17] Alastair Iain Johnston, therefore, disagrees with the realist concept of socialisation represented by the neorealist view of socialisation as a rewarding/punishing mechanism, and states, "Realist socialisation, in fact, is not socialisation either in any standard social science definition or in any common use language sense; it is selection."[18] In reality, however, it is often difficult to distinguish compliant behaviour based on appropriateness from the one based on threat/punishment, or behaviour taken as mandatory from the voluntary. More often than not, an actor socialises itself with what seems forced initially into compliant behaviour by rationalising it as appropriate and valuable.

Some studies on state building, economic reform, and democratisation have touched on state socialisation, too, often by emphasising the human agent's choices, particularly the roles of political leaders at a time of national crisis or regime transition. It is often noted that, in situations of nation building or large-scale economic reform that often involve great turmoil, crises, and tensions, the leaders' role increases in identifying the objectives to be achieved, investigating the major alternative courses of actions, calculating the probable costs and risks as well as the positive consequences of various other alternatives, and searching for new information relevant to assessment of the options. A country's entry into the state system, too, can be regarded as a "constitutive moment," which offers political elites an enormous opportunity to shape the course of events.

Why do states eventually accommodate themselves and accept the universal norms of standard conduct in foreign policy behaviour? Is it the external pressures that force states to comply with international norms? Or do states voluntarily adopt norms by foreseeing the benefit of compliance based on their capacity and will? Do states accept norms out of strategic calculations or out of a sense of obligation? Despite the increased interest in clarifying the precise mechanism of norm diffusion and norm resonance, and despite the increased vocabulary related to norm transmittance such as cascading, learning, framing, grafting, and emulating,[19] we have yet to see a systematic treatment of the subject. Above all, the relationship between social structure and agents is unsolved. The origin of independent variables is also underspecified, and endogeneity has not yet been addressed fully.

In line with many theorists on state socialisation and norm diffusion, I define state socialisation as a country's adjustment process in conforming to the norms of international society. In contrast to the recent "agentic" emphasis on studies that essentially lean towards the voluntarist understanding of state socialisation, I emphasise that states' acceptance of international norms presupposes certain exogenous imperatives/incentives[20] as well as the interpretation and digestion of them on the part of the domestic receivers. State socialisation is not so much a purely designed act on the part of domestic societal groups and political leaders as a phenomenon that lies at the intersection of the international level and the unit level.

Microprocesses: "How" Do States Socialise?

As one of the few attempts to explore the microprocesses of state socialisation, Kai Alderson took up this aspect of state socialisation and discussed the possible contribution that the concept could make to the study of IR.[21] He defines state socialisation as "the process by which states internalise norms arising or arisen elsewhere in the international system." By analysing the process of how international norms become shared by actors, he emphasises the importance of clarifying the mechanisms of the internalisation of norms; that is, the process of how influential economic and political leaders and public leaders change their attitudes, of how domestic actors lobby for compliance with an international norm while sanctioning and punishing violations of them, and of how bureaucratic operating procedures become standard within the society and become institutionalised in accordance with the international norms.[22]

Other scholars have also recognised the inadequacy of attention paid to the microprocesses in the studies on state socialisation. Finnemore and Sikkink, for example, attempt to clarify the "life cycle" of norms by dividing the process into three stages: norm emergence, norm cascade (norm acceptance), and norm internalisation. During the stage of norm emergence, entrepreneurs appear and persuade states to accept a new norm, eventually leading to a tipping point where states adopt the norm. The cascade of norm acceptance is facilitated by states' incentives for conformity, international legitimation, and enhancement of self-esteem, and finally brings the successful outcome of norm internalisation.[23]

On the same theme, Johnston's study on China's participation in international institutions discusses three forms of socialisation as microprocesses that reflect different incentives and degrees of prosocial behaviour of actors: mimicking, social influence, and persuasion. Mimicking, distinguished from emulation, involves borrowing of the common basic rules of the game, such as language, practices, and customs from a new social environment. Social influence reflects actors' "sensitivity" to social status that varies depending on the types of institutions that encourage certain processes of socialisation. While these two forms simply result in behavioural socialisation, persuasion leads to internalisation of a norm, where actors obtain new self-identities and preferences that accord with "logics of apppropriatenss" of the environment.[24]

Microprocesses of state socialisation are difficult to generalise, as they differ depending on the nature of the issues involved in the given norm, the nature of the international environment in which the state is placed, and the stage of socialisation. State socialisation during the entry process into international society is likely to differ from state socialisation of a legitimate member of international society. While the previously mentioned authors discuss socialisation of the actors who have already been recognised as sovereign by international society, the focus of this study is on socialisation of a country striving to gain membership in international society. I hypothesise here that actors go through three stages of socialisation with norms: adoption, absorption, and adaptation. The adoption stage is where actors encounter new norms accompanied by a certain degree of chaos and confusion. The actors confront the task of comprehending and accommodating novel ideas that had been previously alien to them. As the society faces a conflict between traditional domestic institutions and the new ones, this stage is also characterised by slow changes in domestic infrastructures and ideas. Absorption, the second stage, is characterised by vigourous learning, infatuation with the novel, and rapid change. Actors tend to demonstrate flexible and positive attitudes towards the new norms, accelerating the process of their socialisation. The third stage, adaptation, is where actors show increased maturity in their understanding and interpretation of the new norms. They start to take more objective perspectives on the nature and suitability of new ideas and become more selective in what they accept and reject. Actors may even demonstrate a certain cynicism towards the new norms at this stage of socialisation. Each stage of socialisation presents a different range of choices by local actors and their different interests, motivations, and interpretations towards new norms.

I further presuppose that these stages are characterised by three different modes of socialisation, which manifest how the actors reconcile with new norms: the international-dominant mode, the domestic-dominant mode, and the "compartmentalising" mode. Although one of these modes may become more noticeable in a particular stage of socialisation than in another, each stage of state socialisation normally exhibits a mixture of these three modes. In the international-dominant mode, latecomers often abandon their pre-existing domestic institutions in their efforts to accommodate themselves to the dominant international norms. Renouncing the use of native language, which is closely linked to the core of cultural integrity of any society, is one such example. Many non-Western countries in their process of modernisation, in fact, abandoned their native language and adopted a European tongue as their official language. In early Meiji Japan, the governmental officials at one point seriously discussed the possibility of employing English as Japan's official language or writing Japanese in alphabets. Employing foreigners to create entirely new institutions or to introduce new technologies by paying extraordinarily high salaries, as was the case of the national Tomioka silk-reeling factory in Gunma Prefecture in Japan, also belongs to this mode of socialisation.

Socialisees take the domestic-dominant mode when alien norms are easy to absorb due to little discrepancy existing between the international and the domestic institutions, or when external pressures are not strong enough vis-à-vis the level of embedded national identity for the domestic society to alter their norms. In this mode, the newly adopted ideas and institutions are modified and reshaped in ways easily accepted by domestic society; the international is converted to fit the domestic. The most salient example in the case of Japan is translation of Western writings into Japanese. Vigourous translation of numerous Western books faithful to the content of the original text helped the country modernise through its native language and build a new nation based on its old cultural identity.

"Compartmentalisation (segmentalisation)" often characterises the stage where a newcomer meets an alien norm for the first time. Perplexed and confused about how to face and respond to a new norm, the newcomer lets both domestic and international institutions survive and coexist without integrating them into one standard. In the early stage of Japan's encounter with the West, the Japanese often dealt with Westerners based on international law in their language while dealing with the domestic population based on the traditional code of ethics. A country could carry on this mode even after it successfully adopted new norms of international law and was admitted to international society, as it continues to adjust itself to changing imperatives of international environments.

There are many other unresolved issues concerning the microprocesses of state socialisation that call for further reflection. The identification of whether it entails both normative and behavioural compliance or not, for example, is often a source of controversy. In measuring the degree of state socialisation, we should pay attention to the extent of adoption of political, legal, and economic institutions that meet the international standards and promote international norms, such as the country's military system, parlimentary system, educational system, banking system, civil and criminal codes, and participation in international conferences. Also to be considered are the degree of compliance of the prevalent ideas of the contemporary great powers, for example, standards of civilisation, imperialism, and colonialism; national power measured mainly by military and economic strengths; and removal of old political and social traditions. I consider state socialisation as including accommodation to both a normative standard of contemporary international customs, laws, and rules, both explicit and implicit, and a materialistic standard that accords with the required criteria of international society instead of solving the materialist-ideationalist controversy.

The degree of socialisation also needs to be measured in light of the degree of consolidation of international society, as state socialisation presupposes the existence of an international society, first of all. The degree of socialisation of one country is related to how much "society" there is and in what way a system is institutionalised at the international level. If international relations form a "tight" society with enmeshed ties and channels among countries, and with extensiverules and norms, for example, the countries within such an international system are necessarily required to demonstrate a higher degree of engagement in order to be called "socialised." If the international system remains "loose," just an occasional diplomatic exchange with other countries might suffice for a country to be recognised as "socialised." It is crucial, therefore, to discuss socialisation not only from the level of the agent's attributes, but from the international society level as well. With European empowerment and expansion throughout the globe, the sovereign state system as an institution became "tighter" in the nineteenth century, increasing the level of socialising pressure on newcomer states. The degree of institutionalisation of the international system was, thus, a question tied to a country's degree of socialisation.[25]

Theories of Institutions and Institutionalisation

Sovereign State System and International Law as Institutions

While the study of institutions has occupied the central locus of political science, the foci of the study have been considerably transformed over time. In the early period, the study focused on formal administrative structures, procedures, and functions, or rules and laws of political institutions. Focus gradually shifted from formal attributes of political institutions to informal ones starting in the 1950s, when scholars began identifying some behavioural patterns of institutions. In the 1970s, the study of institutions was revived as new institutionalism, where the dynamic nature of institutions was conceptualised in a theoretically more meaningful way than before through the analysis of their origins and causes of change. The contribution of the economic historian Douglass North[26] was applied widely to other social sciences. In the field of IR, for example, the development of theories of regimes in the 1980s and international institutions later on owed much to the concepts and logic that North originally developed. In the field of comparative politics, institutionalism was applied to comparative analysis of the political-economic system of a country. Furthermore, new institutionalism was applied to explain state building, and used in analysing the emergence and transformation of sovereign states and international systems.[27]

As is noted in North's definition of institutions as "a set of rules, compliance procedures, and moral and ethical behavioural norms designed to constrain the behaviour of individuals in the interests of maximising the wealth or utility of principals,"[28] institutions entail two aspects that can be contradictory to each other. On the one hand, actors voluntarily create institutions, reflecting their preferences and interests; on the other, once created, institutions constrain the behaviour of actors and the relations among them. In fact, different institutionalist scholars define institutions differently, varying from those who emphasise the institutional constraints on actors to those who emphasise the institutional dynamics where actors' intentions are considered as a major force in institutional creation and transformation. As an example of the former, James March and Johan Olsen define institutions as "a relatively stable collection of practices and rules defining appropriate behaviour of specific groups of actors in specific situations."[29] As a latter example, William Riker mentions that "institutions are no more than rules and rules are themselves the product of social decisions. Consequently the rules are also not in equilibrium."[30] How to conceptualise the balance between actors' voluntarism and institutional autonomy is a key to understanding institutions and is also a focus of future studies on institutions.[31] It has been increasingly recognised among scholars that the interaction between the systemic/societal constraints and the choices that actors make is one of the unexplored areas in the institutionalist literature. [32]

The sovereign state system can be considered as an institution that entails certain rules and norms designed to constrain the behaviour of states. It provides a political order based on territorial borders, excluding any higher authority within a given territory. Noninterference and self-help have been two basic principles of the sovereign state system as an institution since the Treaty of Westphalia. International law is also an institution that can be simultaneously conceived of as a subinstitution of the sovereign state system and as an embodiment of it. It can be defined as "a miscellaneous aggregate of rules, principles, procedures, decision, orders, policies, precedents, and other normative elements."[33] International law, in other words, is an institution that reflects general patterns or customary behaviour in international relations. Kal Holsti states that international law is "an important institution of international politics. Indeed, it is so important that it distinguishes a society of states from a conglomeration of independent political units."[34] Similarly, E. H. Carr notes that the existence of international law presupposes the existence of international society and that, in the case of international law, the power element makes its function more "political" than in the case of domestic law.[35]

As an institution, international law has certain functions to perform: ensuring mutual independence of states, promoting or discouraging certain international norms of the day, and socialising latecomers. Bull examined the roles of international law as one of the institutions in international society, identifying three functions of international law in relation to "order" in international society. First, international law identifies the idea of a society of sovereign states. Second, international law states the basic rules of coexistence among states and other actors in international society. Third, international law facilitates compliance with the rules of international society by "providing a means by which states can advertise their intentions with regard to the matter in question," providing "reassurance" about the future policies of states, and "solemnising the agreement" so as to create an expectation of permanence. What is implied here overlaps the functions that institutionalists in American IR literature identify, such as "information provision," "transaction cost reduction," "increased transparency," and "the shadow of the future."[36]

Institutionalisation Dynamics

Many of the core elements of institutional dynamism are contained in Huntington's concept of institutionalisation. His model helps us theorise how institutions originate, stabilise, and transform, and can be applied to the analysis of the European sovereign state system. In exploring institutional dynamics, it is useful to re-examine the concept of institutionalisation that was originally developed by Huntington, but has been obliterated in the political science literature for a long time. Huntington examined the importance of political institutions in relation to political development and conceptualised political institutions as something that mitigated or avoided conflicts among different social forces that accompany modernisation and social mobilisation. Defining institutionalisation as "the process by which organisations and procedures acquire value and stability,"[37] he also stated that political institutionalisation that accords with the level of social and economic change is necessary for political stability and listed four criteria for institutionalisation: adaptability, complexity, autonomy, and coherence.[38]

In the process of institutionalisation of certain norms and rules, a general pattern is observed where those norms and rules acquire exclusive characteristics that can distinguish them from others. In this pattern, norms and rules exist for a certain period of time, stabilise, and then transform, responding to environmental stimuli. Also involved in the process are actors' perceptions of institutional constraints and adjustment to those constraints, all of which contribute to institutional survival and stability. Further, institutions themselves incorporate extraneous elements, contributing to their higher degree of complexity and adaptability. From the essence of Huntington's arguments, I deduce that "autonomy" and "adaptability" are the most fundamental aspects of institutionalisation. The former makes an institution emerge independently from others and establish its intrinsic identity. The latter contributes to adding flexibility and complexity that helps an institution interact with the environment smoothly and survive for a long period of time.

"Autonomy" is related to "coherence" in Huntington's analysis. It is a criterion that measures institutional constraints on actors. In the first phase of institutionalisation, institutions acquire "autonomy," providing actors with coherent rules and behavioural appropriateness. A political system develops certain distinct characteristics of its own that can clearly separate it from other political entities. With rules that distinguish some institutions from others and with the rationale for those rules, institutions make it possible for actors to directly and specifically predict possible interactions with others and lead actors to adjust themselves to institutional rules in an appropriate manner. When an institution's membership suddenly expands, the institution can easily lose its coherence. An autonomous political institution, however, obliges its members to comply with rules, and maintains coherence without losing its institutional integrity.[39] "The greater the conformity between behaviour and institutional rules, the higher the level of institutionalization."[40] An autonomous institution can also neutralise or eliminate the influence of new members by delaying newcomers' joining the system or changing their attitudes and behaviours through the process of political socialisation.

In the second phase of institutionalisation, an institution acquires adaptability, which is related to another of Huntington's criteria, complexity, and concerns institutional survival and stability. Complex institutions with many purposes and roles tend to absorb new social forces and members by integrating actors' preferences easily, since, even when a subunit's purpose is lost, other purposes of other subunits can easily compensate. Therefore, a complex institution has strong adaptability to its environment. Adaptability means two things. One is an ability to endure extensive environmental changes. Institutions that have endured and survived environmental challenges can be considered to have higher degrees of adaptability. The second meaning is an ability to increase its supporter-members and adopt foreign elements. Although Huntington placed emphasis on an institution's longevity as its measure of adaptability, the spatial breadth that an institution covers on the globe is also an important criterion. An adaptable institution has the flexibility to incorporate outlandish elements of new members not only without sacrificing institutional autonomy and stability, but also in a way to give itself more autonomy and stability.

In short, institutional autonomy works as constraints on actors, and institutional adaptability indicates the ability to accommodate actors' attributes. In this sense, the dynamics between institutions and actors mentioned in the discussions of socialisation again become the central theme of institutionalisation. This theoretical framework to conceptualise institutionalisation from the point of view of institutional autonomy and adaptability is helpful in examining the process of expansion and development of the European international system as it gradually absorbed countries that had belonged to different civilisations and political systems. A high degree of compliance of newcomers led to further survival and autonomy of the international system as an institution, as encounters with countries of different cultural and civilisational backgrounds highlighted the European identity of state relations. At the same time, in the process of engaging different actors, the European state system became a more complex system with more capability and flexibility to adapt to the new environment. Actors' accommodation, in other words, further institutionalised the sovereign state-system.

Newcomers' socialisation occurred in parallel with institutionalisation of the European sovereign state system.

The Evolution of the International System and Law

A common understanding of the modern international system and international law is that it originated in the seventeenth-century Europe and was consolidated during the nineteenth century.[41] The history of the modern European state system and international law can be divided into three stages of development: the creation of the Westphalian system during the seventeenth century, the emergence of Eurocentric international society with the European norm of the "standard of the civilisation" in the nineteenth century, and the globalisation of the state system and democratisation of the legal/external sense of sovereignty since decolonisation in the latter half of the twentieth century. Each stage presented a form of universalism, periodising the history of modern international relations: "At first the world was destined to become Christian, then it was destined to become civilised, while now it is destined to become legally egalitarian (but not at all materially)."[42] Transformations from each of these steps to another have entailed changes in the concept of statehood, in the criteria for membership in the international society, and in the norms that bound the members. Each of these transformations also presupposed some exogenous changes that led to the institutional adaptation of the international system. Examination of the characteristics of the three big transformations observed in the history of the sovereign state system enlightens us on the particular historic era in which Japan's entry into international society and its modern state building took place in the history of the European international system from the perspective of institutional change.

The Westphalian Transformation

The emergence of the sovereign state system in Europe was a phenomenal event that marked the start of modern international relations. Military revolution and the increased degree of economic interdependence are identified as exogenous factors that precipitated the creation of a new institution called the Westphalian international system. As an institution, the system operated from the basis of two principles of sovereignty: internal hierarchy and external independence, which implied that the nature of interstate relations was anarchical.

There are many studies that focus on state building in Western Europe and the emergence of the international system in the seventeenth century.[43] Charles Tilly and Hendrik Spruyt, in particular, offer insightful explanations for the creation of states and state-systems from different angles. Tilly claims European state building occurreed because military competition brought about by the military revolution at the end of the Middle Ages served as an exogenous factor for the institutional change.[44] Starting around 1400, the invention of artillery, modern fortifications, and massed infantry, in particular, increased the need to secure revenue from society to maintain the security of a political entity. Although military competition drove the European states in the same general direction of state building, countries differed in how they combined the two social logics, military (coercive) and economic (capital), widening the gap in power among states. States that efficiently used both "coercive intensive" and "capital intensive" methods proved better at waging war and dominating the poorer, less urbanised areas in Europe. Since the 1970s, Tilly has been faithful to his original thesis: "States made war and war made states."[45] He studied the state's ability to raise revenue from its citizens for war and regarded war as the primary state activity. For Tilly, the essence of European state building was the security capability of a political entity, which was also the source of institutional selection in international politics.

Spruyt examined the origin of the state and state system during the period between 1000 and 1648 with the aim of refining and modifying Tilly's arguments. He suggests that the emergence of the sovereign state system in Europe can be explained by the functional ability of the state to respond to the increased degree of economic interdependence and commercial development that occurred at the end of the Middle Ages. According to Spruyt, therefore, it was economic, not military, competition, that led to the victory of the sovereign state, superseding city-leagues and city-states as synchronic alternatives. By establishing a central authority, sovereign states could prevent free riding, to reduce transaction costs, and to rationalise the economy by standardising coinage, weights, and measurements. By mobilising social resources, they were thereby recognised as the legitimate actors in international relations. Spruyt is also influenced by Gould's theory of punctuated equilibrium, [46]explaining institutional changes by institutional selection that occurs as a response to major environmental changes. For him, the major environmental change that occurred during the eleventh through thirteenth centuries was the growth in commerce and economic expansion that transformed the relative position and powers of different social groups. Spruyt uses institutional theories more consciously than Tilly by combining grand theory, bargaining, and the perspective of evolution. While military efficiency had been considered the standard explanation for the emergence of states since Tilly, Spruyt introduced economic efficiency as the source of institutional selection.[47]

At this stage of history, under the broad exogenous transformation of military revolution and economic interdependence, it was essentially the internal dimensions of states that defined the external dimensions of statehood and the qualification for membership in international society. In order to remain a member of international society, a state had to have solved its internal problems, including coherence and solidarity as a nation, effective jurisdiction, and creation of loyal citizens to fight for the good of their country. *De facto* sovereignty was a precondition for *de jure* sovereignty.

The Positivist Transformation

While the core functions of the European sovereign state system as an institution have themselves been resistant to change, shifts in broad socioeconomic or political context brought changes to its "subinstitutions," including international law and its norms. These subinstitutions have shaped the meanings and functioning of the sovereign state system for particular historical periods. European empowerment and its concomitant geographical expansion in the eighteenth and nineteenth centuries, for example, gave rise to special norms of the period: a "concert of Europe," a "standard of civilisation," "nationalism," and "national interest." European state systems during these periods possessed institutional structures, functions, and norms that distinguished them from international systems in different periods of history.

If institutional changes are usually brought about by changes in both socioeconomic and political contexts, the Industrial Revolution that started in seventeenth-century Britain was an important exogenous factor in the socioeconomic context that dramatically raised the material standard of Europe to an incomparable degree in relation to other international societies. The material empowerment of Europe led to its concomitant expansion abroad, bringing significant political consequences. The nineteenth century was the age of science, the age of the Victorian ideals of progress, optimism, and liberalism.[48] Industry and technology were considered instruments for the betterment and progress of human society. It was also a period when international law transformed from natural law to positive law, changing the concept of sovereignty to a substantive one based on the historical experiences and actual power that a state possesses, not on a universally shared sense of morality. "[The] vocabulary of international law could not be separated ... from the material conditions of industrializing industrialising capitalism"[49] of the era.

Since the mid-nineteenth century, the formalities and techniques of international law have undergone revolutionary changes. Such changes entailed the establishment of various international organisations, development of the law of war, developments in the procedures of international arbitration and mediation, including the establishment of the Permanent Court of Arbitration in 1899, legalisation of property rights and issues of shipping, and efforts to curtail piracy, buccaneers, and mercenary activities. Further, the nineteenth century witnessed an increased sense of nationalism and changes in the conduct of war, which accompanied a change in the way military power was employed as a means to pursue national policies. These phenomena all occurred in parallel, each intrinsically related to one another. They were related parts of the transformation that international society has undergone since the Industrial Revolution.

Paul Schroeder points out that European international relations changed dramatically from an "international system" to an "international society" between 1763 and 1848 with the emergence of the exclusive concept called "Europe."[50] The international system up to the turn of the nineteenth century was what Watson calls "inclusive international society,"[51] where the power gap between the European and non-European states remained relatively small, enabling European countries to establish relations with others as equal partners. The concept of Europe as an exclusive society of the most civilised nation states, however, gradually took over, changing the criteria for membership in international society and giving rise to Eurocentric international norms.

Since the middle of the nineteenth century, the recognition of a state has come to depend more on subjective domestic factors than an abstract, universal morality. In the nineteenth century, international law became "an expression of the will of the state, and ... used by those who control the state as an instrument of coercion against those who oppose their power. The law is therefore the weapon of the stronger."[52] The nature and the objective of states thus became more important criteria for membership in international society during this period than at any other time in history. The determination of who was "to be admitted into international society, to what extent, and for what purposes"[53] came to depend on this new sense of sovereignty. Turning away from natural law to positive international law, international lawyers during this era also based their rules of conduct on the actual body of custom and treaties that were historically accumulated. During this "positivist" era, the contact between Europe and non-European powers ceased to be equal.[54]

Legal positivism bridged the gap between the European and non-European powers by the explicit imposition of European international law over the "uncivilised" non-Europeans. Legal positivism meant, first, that sovereignty was the supreme authority to enforce laws and rules. Second, law was considered the creation of the sovereign states that regulate relations between them. Third, the actual behaviour of states that create rules and institutions became the basis of international law. This was a significant contrast to thinking based on natural law, where sovereign states were considered to be bound by an overarching higher morality.[55]

This positivist turn is often called the emergence of a "realist view of international law,"[56] explicitly mentioned first by Jean Bodin and Thomas Hobbes much earlier. "*Ius ést quod ius sum est* [law is the command of the sovereign]"[57] was the idea where law was entirely cut off from ethics and became something that an authority enforces. Countries that aspired to obtain membership in international society, therefore, had to meet the European standards of adherence to international law, which included the capacity to observe the rules in diplomatic relations, protection of people's basic rights, and an efficient domestic administration system, to name a few. Depending on the degree to which these standards were met, membership in international society was designated as full, partial, or nonexistent.

Until the end of the eighteenth century Europe was not strong enough to resort to threats in dealing with other international societies or states. Empowered Europe, however, gained the ability to exercise direct control over many parts of the world. As a consequence, meeting the "standard" and increasing national power became the foremost agenda of all the non-European states that were to enter international society. In 1856, Turkey became the first country to pass the test of the "standard of civilisation" and entered Eurodominant international society by being invited to participate in major international conferences.[58] Countries that failed the test were subject to activities such as territorial partition, unequal treaties, invasion, and opening of ports by the European powers. Non-European countries had to concede to these measures.

The "standard of civilisation" involved all aspects of domestic and international life. First, the norms of liberal European civilisation needed to be met. They included guaranteed basic rights and respect for life, liberty, dignity of the individual, property, freedom of travel, commerce, and religion, as well as abstention from practices such as polygamy, slavery, and suttee. Second, effective political organisation, especially an organised, honest, efficient political bureaucracy possessed with the ability to defend itself against external aggression, needed to be established. Third, internal and external law systems, including maintenance of independent domestic courts, publicised civil and criminal codes that guaranteed legal justice for native and foreign nationals within the jurisdiction, and a constitution, were called for. Fourth, "civilised" countries were required to engage in diplomatic intercourse and communication through participation at international conferences and adherence to international law. Fifth, they needed to conform to Western habits and customs of clothes and diet. [59] The standard needed to be exercised both domestically and externally, materialistically and normatively, in positive and negative senses, explicitly and implicitly.

Some of the criteria for the "standard," however, could be recognised more objectively than others. Unspoken assumptions were often also an integral part of the standard. In such a situation, great powers frequently recognised the qualification of newcomers according to "the powerful and unpredictable expedience of competition for colonies."[60] The status of the non-European countries, therefore, remained ambiguous and subjective despite their actual qualification for international personality.[61] Discretion on the part of the European powers in deciding who has passed the test, therefore, was a big hurdle that Japan and other non-European powers faced in the process of socialisation. Newcomers sometimes needed to surpass the standards of the dominant powers in order to provetheir worthiness for membership. The standard of civilisation was in many ways tested by how much "might" a country possessed. Materialistic power, both economic and military, came to be a measurement of a country's success in meeting the European standard of the family of nations. "Might" indeed became "right."

> The nineteenth-century shift toward positive law and the tendency to describe civilized rights on a threat basis gave a new name to an old

> practice – the willingness to use military force when basic rights, as defined by European conceptions of international law, were perceived to have been denied.... What changed was not so much the European willingness to use force to impose a standard of civilization as the European ability to do so. Increasing use of European military force against non-European countries coincided with increasing availability of superior European fire-power.[62]

The political implication of the positivist turn to international law was, thus, significant, as it rationalised the use of force against non-European countries and justified the ability and the employment of military force.

The "standard of civilisation" also functioned as a guarantee of certain basic rights in often hostile foreign lands to protect the lives, liberty, and property of the Europeans in non-European lands, as European countries expanded into other areas of the globe, creating problems.[63] It was in many ways an *ad hoc* invention applied to non-European countries inconsistently in justification of European domination. From the perspectives of the property rights arguments, the "standard" provided a rationale for an institutional arrangement to divide up the remaining land on the globe as property rights by limiting international recognition to candidate states. As the physical expansion of Europe meant a gradual decrease in space on the globe, some kind of new institutional arrangements became necessary. Here, "transaction cost" was reduced by the international norm of colonialism, which was another side of the coin of the "standard of civilisation." It was in this context of European dominance and the rise of the "standard of civilisation" that Japan faced its agenda for modern state building.

Since the way law and political community operate is defined by time and space in the particular historical period, the timing of a country's entry into international society plays a significant role in deciding the way it socialises within the norms and rules of international society. In Part II, I examine the process whereby Japan, confronting the socialising pressure to conform to Western international law at the initial stage of its encounter with the West, gradually learned to use the system for its national interests and development, in parallel with its efforts to acquire membership in international society. As outlined here, this process took place under the overarching normative structure of the age of positivism and robust imperialism.

PART TWO

The Process of Conformity

3 Adoption: Introduction of International Law, 1853–1860s

As we undertake our historical case study of Japan's socialisation into the international system, the first issue that we come across is that of periodisation. Many events occur in parallel incessantly in history. By periodising history, we necessarily assume that changes have occurred, when in fact the past exhibits a seamless fabric that does not allow any sharp line to be drawn. While dividing Japan's socialisation process into three convenient time periods makes the process more intelligible, each historical event is, in fact, tied to the others. Certain events or accumulation of public energy towards some cause in one historical period may affect events in another. Periodising history, therefore, is "necessarily a theoretical activity,"[1] as it provides frameworks to interpret and reconstitute events by identifying continuity and change.

Besides the issue of grouping historical periods itself, how to group poses another problem. I will divide the period of investigation loosely into three according to Japan's changing attitudes towards the West as follows: 1853–1860s, 1870s, and 1880s–1899. The first phase of Japan's socialisation in this study that covers the period from the arrival in 1853 of Commodore Matthew C. Perry to the end of the 1860s is when Japan started to engage in the international society dominated by the West, while gradually overcoming the political rivalry between domains (*han*) and fostering a sense of national unity. It was an era of chaos, even though Japan's encounter with the West was moderate in nature compared with that of other newcomer states. In this era of norm "adoption," the law of nations was introduced to Japan as a general treatise to be translated and studied. This period is characterised by the slow change in society, while the second phase, the 1870s (covered in Chapter 4), features a rapid change. The 1870s was a turning point, when Japan started to clearly direct its course towards building a modern state after the overthrow of the Tokugawa *bakufu*,[2] which gave the momentum for an enormous transformation of the society. Under an entirely new political system, Japan opened up to and started to "absorb" the Western norms of international society vigourously. The third and last phase covers the period from the early 1880s to 1899, the period of norm "adaptation," when Japanese understanding of international law gradually matured, enabling the leaders to see different shades and nuances of international law. Political leaders had graduated from the naïve infatuation with Western civilisation that had characterised the previous era by then and had become more realistic in their dealing with international law and with other countries. They gradually learned to adapt and use the international law for the enhancement of national interests, culminating in Japan's formal acquisition of an international status as a civilised nation by the abrogation of extraterritoriality after a series of negotiations and efforts to appeal to the West.

This chapter starts with a brief overview of the international environment in which Japan was situated before the arrival of the West and a short discussion on the nature of the European approach to Asian countries, followed by a sketch of how Japan met with the requests of the West and accepted international law.

The Asian Encounter with the West

The Asian Interstate System

Two international systems are known to have existed in ancient Asia: a Sinocentric system and an Indian international system. Japan at least for a short time belonged to the Sinocentric system, although its degree of immersion in the system remains debatable. Since ancient times, Japan had learned a lot from Chinese culture by sending embassies there, especially during the Tang and Ming dynasties. The political social system that developed in Japan, however, was quite different from that of China. Japan had never been under direct political control of China as countries that were not separated by the sea from China such as Vietnam or Korea had been. The Chinese system has changed considerably throughout different phases of history. Relations with other countries showed more equality or inequality at some times than at other times. The content of the relations with China differed from country to country, too. Japan's interaction with China in general tended to be contained at the minimum.

The international system that centred around China was based on Confucianism. Hierarchy was the natural order in the Confucian concept of the world. Conquest of other people ought to be achieved by civilisation and virtue and not by coercion. Use of military force, therefore, was traditionally denied. China's superiority as the centre of the world was the core value in the system. Countries that existed outside the Chinese civilisation were considered barbaric and could not conclude interstate ties with "civilised" countries in the Chinese sense. The Confucian Chinese international system was further extended by civilising the barbarians. The essential characteristics of the Chinese system, which prospered until the European empowerment, in other words, was hierarchy and inequality among states.[3]

The major interactions between China and other states took the form of a tributary and investiture system. Tributaries recognised China's superiority; in return, China recognised the independence of the tributaries and did not intervene in their domestic affairs, even if China retained the right to do so. The Sinocentric international system was divided into three regions: Sinic zone, which consists of Korea, Vietnam, and Ryukyu[4]; Asian zone that includes Tibet and other inland areas; and outer zone consisting of Southeast and South Asia, Japan, and the West. The Chinese system lasted until the arrival of the West in the nineteenth century.[5]

THE ARRIVAL OF THE WEST

While the early contact of Asian countries with the West was based on more or less equal relations, it started to take on the characteristics of Western political intervention into East Asia from around the beginning of the nineteenth century. China for the next 100 years lost its influence over tributary states, suffered political, commercial and territorial damages, and was deprived of the status as an international actor. The Opium War from 1840 to 1842 was the decisive event that demonstrated European superiority of power. The Western invasion eventually meant first, the end of the Chinese international system in East Asia, second, the rise of Japan, and third, the change in the political units in Asia into nation states and integration of Asia into a global international system dominated by the West.

Initially, European powers had to approach Asian countries differently from their American and African counterparts. In America and

Africa, Europeans took an approach of domination, either by majority or minority control. Europeans, however, approached Asian states more as "clients." Although they did not recognise Asian states as subjects of international law in the full European sense, their territory at least was not considered as subject to foreign occupation as was the case with Africa, America, and Australia.[6] The Europeans had first established diplomatic relations with Asian powers and the reciprocal relations continued up to the nineteenth century. From the perspective of sovereignty as control over territory and possession of "property rights over definite portions of the earth's surface," many Asian states had met the definition of sovereignty. From the perspective of the *de facto* sense of sovereignty, or the capability of the sovereign that exercises effective control over the society, however, Asian states had met with suspicion. With the empowerment of Europe during the nineteenth century in parallel with the development of positivist international law, the legal personality of Asian countries came to be questioned. When the exclusive great power concert was established with the Congress of Vienna in 1815, the major European powers took the entire authority to define membership on themselves as "guardians" and "executive directors" of the Eurodominant international community.[7] International legal status of countries in the world thus came to be at the mercy of the claim made by those European powers, who admitted or denied the birth of new states and death of the existing states at their will, often irrespective of the reality of statehood.[8]

> The positivist attempt to distinguish between the civilized and uncivilized was fraught with unresolved complications. ... but these [complications] were irrelevant in terms of the broad issue of the central distinction between the civilized and uncivilized. The international law of the period can be read, not simply as the confident expansion of intellectual imperialism, but a far more anxiety-driven process of naming the unfamiliar, asserting its alien nature, and attempting to reduce and subordinate it ... The whole edifice of positivist jurisprudence is based on these initial exclusions and discriminations. [9]

Asian states and their civilisation came to be reduced, for the first time in their history, from the status of full international membership to the status of ambiguity. In the era of positive international law, when international society became identical with the Concert of Europe, they became candidates competing for European-defined full membership, to which the international law would be applicable.[10] The power configuration of the globe had changed, allowing the European powers to exercise colonial rules based on their actual power backed by the positivist international law that rationalised it. Countries in Asia were among those countries that could not participate in the development of the international law during this period of great transformation. Europe alone retained the authority to play an active role in the institutionalisation of the international law.[11] How did Japan, which entered the international system at this particular time period of high imperialism of the latter half of the nineteenth century as a newcomer, acknowledge the institutional constraints of the international society and adapt itself? In the following, I will turn to the process of Japan's accommodation to the nineteenth-century international law as an actor's response to such institutional constraints.

Perry's Arrival and After

As we have seen, the European approach to Asian countries was not that of conquer and control as in the case of Africa, America, and Australia. By the Eurocentric "standard of civilisation," countries such as Turkey, China, Thailand (then called Siam), and Japan were grouped in a "semicivilised" category, which was distinguished from the "uncivilised." For several reasons, the Western approach to Japan above all was gentle and peaceful, even compared with other countries categorised as "semicivilised." First, Japan's encounter with the West was delayed. The simple geographical unattractiveness of Japan as a target of Western political objectives had spared Japan hostility and conflict with the West, while the sheer size of China, for example, attracted the West. For European powers the question of how to deal with Asia centred around the question of how to deal with China, a country with great civilisation but politically weak. Moreover, having met with strong resistance previously in China, India, and Turkey before coming to Japan, the Western countries did not show as much colonial enthusiasm towards Japan as towards those countries. Therefore, "no wars were fought, no smuggling trade developed, no territory was forfeited. Not a single man was killed on either side during Perry's expedition to Japan, and the commercial treaties were negotiated amicably around a table."[12]

Second, Japan's first encounter with the West was with the United States, whose interest was more commercial than that of the colonial-minded Europeans. The US objective was made clear in the annual message to Congress by President Millard Fillmore:

> The waters of the Northern Pacific, even into the Arctic Sea, have of late years been frequented by our whalemen. The application of steam to the general purposes of navigation is becoming daily more common, and makes it desirable to obtain fuel and other necessary supplies at convenient points on the route between Asia and our Pacific shores. Our unfortunate countrymen who from time to time suffer shipwreck on the coasts of the eastern seas are entitled to protection. Besides these specific objects, the general prosperity of our States in the Pacific requires that an attempt should be made to open the opposite regions of Asia to a mutually beneficial intercourse. It is obvious that this attempt could be made by no power to so great advantage as by the United States, whose constitutional system excludes every idea of distant colonial dependencies. I have accordingly been led to order an appropriate naval force to Japan, under the command of a discreet and intelligent officer of the highest rank known to our service. He is instructed to endeavor to obtain from the Government of that country some realization of the inhospitable and anti-social system which it has pursued for about two centuries.[13]

The supply of fuel, protection at the time of shipwreck, and mutually beneficial relations were exactly what Perry demanded from Japan in a letter that President Fillmore ordered him to hand to the emperor. The letter also stated that "the Constitution and laws of the United States forbid all interference with the religions or political concerns of other nations."[14]

Third, as Westerners had obtained information about the Japanese resilience as a nation during the several centuries before Perry's arrival,[15] they showed somewhat more prudent attitudes in dealing with Japan than in the case of other Asian countries. Although Japan adopted a policy of isolation (*sakoku*) in 1638, Europeans had reached Japan since the sixteenth century, leaving records of what they had observed of the Far Eastern country in diaries and books.[16] Some had learned about the characteristics of the spirited Japanese soldiers and came to believe that they would not be able to defeat them in the case of the long land war. *Histoire de l'eglise du Japon*, written by Jean Crasset in 1689, for example, illustrates the Western perception of the Japanese soldiers vividly, touching on the appalling sharpness of the Japanese sword, which from the age of twelve Japanese men always wear at the waist. In describing the Japanese character, he emphasises their belief in honour and hatred to be looked down on, stating that the courage, spiritedness, quickness, curiosity, perception, and the diligence of the Japanese could bear all kinds of sufferings and battle.[17] As another example, Ernest Satow, a British interpreter who came to Japan at the end of the nineteenth century, is known to have warned Harry Parks, a highly successful British diplomat who had served in China before coming to Japan, that the bluffing techniques that worked in China when negotiating would not work with the Japanese.[18]

Perry arrived in Uraga on July 8, 1853. From the experience of Captain James Biddle, who had come to Edo Bay in 1846, but was refused entry and withdrew without negotiating the opening of relations between the two countries, he was more prepared to strongly demand the opening up of Japan "as a right, and not as a favour."[19] The news of Perry's arrival immediately spread all over Japan. It is said that, within two weeks from his arrival, everybody in Japan knew about it, thanks to an excellent information-delivering system of "*hikyaku*," or "flying legs" literally, originated in the Kamakura period and developed extensively during the Edo period.

Over the course of two hundred years, the *bakufu*'s control had extended to cover the whole of Japan. Japan was already possessed with an effective social system to gather information, if the analysis of the information may have been something beyond its capacity at that time. Facing domestic turmoil and sick of the inefficient bureaucracy, one of the capable shogunate leaders (*rōju*), Abe Masahiro, thought that he should let all the *daimyos* (feudal nobles or lords) in Japan know of the content of the letter from the US president and share the peril that the government was facing. By publicising the president's letter to everyone in Japan, Abe aimed at building consensus and uniting Japan, giving the people a sense of danger, while at the same time preparing for the worst, or for fighting against the West.[20] In response to the letter's publication, Abe received 177 petitions, which contained various ideas on how to meet the challenge from the West, including the fortification of Edo, trading with China, and gathering wealth to prepare for the coming fight against the West. Among the petitions, 47 percent were against the opening of Japan and only 4 percent supported it. At this point, the *bakufu* decided to undertake a "*burakashi*" (procrastination) policy, delaying its decisions on how to respond to the Western demand.[21] For the next several years, vigourous responses came from all over Japan, even from residents of cities remote from the capital.[22]

When Perry came back the following year, on February 12, 1854, he came deeply into the bay, ignoring Japan's demand not to pass the line to enter Edo Bay, and in Kurihama, handed over a letter from the president, demanding replenishment of their stocks of coal and provisions, arrangements for the proper treatment of shipwrecked sailors, and opening of the country for commercial relations. He further entered close to Kawasaki, panicking the Japanese and maintaining his heavy-handed stance during the negotiations. He demanded that Japan open three ports, which Japan refused to do at first. Japan eventually had to concede to open two ports, Shimoda and Hakodate, as well as to agree to protect wrecked ships and to replenish fuels and provisions. The treaty, which became the first break of Japan's seclusion policy, was called the Treaty of Peace and Amity or the Treaty of Kanagawa. At this time, opening the two ports did not mean opening commercial relations at all. No provisions for extraterritoriality were made, either, although a most-favoured-nation (MFN) clause was included, securing the possible privileges granted to other countries to the United States.

Perry's arrival was the beginning of the breakdown of the *bakufu* and the reunification of Japan. The threat it posed and the peril that Japan felt revealed the weakness of the *bakufu*'s control. Japan came to need help from all the *daimyos* in the country in order to protect itself. With Perry's arrival, the Japanese started to identify themselves not with domains under each *daimyo*, but with Japan as an entity that would eventually be called a nation. A sense of unity had been created during the two hundred years of Tokugawa rule, at least at the unconscious level, which could be easily transformed into the concept of a nation with the arrival of the West. The geographical fact that it was a relatively small, island country with good accessibility among islands, and the extensive nationwide networks of communication and transportation facilitated Japan's responsiveness and national coherence.

Within a short time, the Japanese came to perceive their country as facing a great change. Abe's effort to spread the news of Perry was the first instance of a Japanese leader using a foreign threat to lead the country in a better direction. Publicising the US president's letter and asking a nationwide audience for opinions on itwas something that nobody had thought of before. It is also notable that Abe received many responses from all over Japan, some of which came from intellectuals equipped with accurate knowledge of the West and concerned with the future of Japan.

While the Japanese encounter with the West was rather gentle compared with the case of China, Japan demonstrated much stronger responsiveness with quick and determined reorganisation of the country that would meet the standard of modern international power. Its less violent encounter with the West and its greater response remain a paradox to many.

Unequal Treaties and Extraterritoriality

When American minister Townsend Harris arrived in 1858, the Treaty of Amity and Commerce, or the Treaty of Shimoda, was concluded with two major "inequalities" contained in it: tariff restrictions and extraterritoriality. Due to these two provisions, Japan was left limited in its sovereignty as an independent state. Between the two "inequalities," the political leaders initially considered the former as more fundamental, since tariff autonomy was a must to promote industrialisation and modernisation. In fact, the foreign ministers who came to be in charge of treaty negotiations in the later period, such as Terajima, Inoue, and Ōkuma, tended to trade continued Western extraterritorial privileges for lifting of the inequality of fixed tariffs.[23] The general public, however, focused their attention more on extraterritoriality, which had more symbolic significance and concerned national pride and honour.

Extraterritoriality can be defined as "the extension of jurisdiction by a state beyond its own borders."[24] Extraterritoriality was first introduced to East Asia after the Opium War with the Treaty of Nanjing in 1842, between China and Britain. Treaty ports were established so that the foreigners could claim immunity from the jurisdiction of the local courts and be tried under the laws of their own countries and under the jurisdiction of their own consuls. For the Western countries, extraterritoriality was to provide their nationals with respect for life, liberty, and property rights in foreign lands where they were not always guaranteed. Governed only by the laws of their countries, foreigners enjoying extraterritorial rights could freely obtain land or engage in commercial activities. In China, the number of such treaty ports increased to eighty-five by the end of the nineteenth century.[25]

According to Jones, extraterritoriality "finds its origin in a concept of law which is as old as the most primitive of societies."

> The belief that the stranger within the gates should be judged according to his own law and not by that of the people among whom he resides is much

> older than the contrary axiom of the territoriality of law, which is largely derived from the comparatively modern theory of sovereignty. In ancient times law was universally held to be personal in nature since it was a crystallization of customs which were inextricably interwoven with religious beliefs and ceremonies. Participation in legal rights and obligations was an integral part of citizenship which could not possibly be extended to the alien, no matter what the cultural standard of his city or tribe might be.... Thus the Turks, when at the zenith of their power, granted extraterritorial privileges with a lavish hand, and permitted their exercise even when they had not been conferred by treaty. For the Ottomans, in common with most oriental races, still considered law as personal rather than as territorial in character and were not conscious of any infringement of their sovereign powers by the exemption of a few alien traders from their jurisdiction ... Originally, therefore, the feeling of superiority, in so far as it existed at all, was on the side of the power which conceded extraterritorial rights.[26]

For the same reason, Japan was more than generous in giving extraterritorial privileges to the Westerners when the first Europeans,starting with the Portuguese in 1542, reached Japan. As law and justice for the Japanese was more personal than territorial in nature in the feudal tradition based rather on the personal tie between the *daimyō* and the retainer (*samurai*) than on landholding as in the West, they demonstrated the same willingness as the Ottoman Sultans "to grant exemption from the native jurisdiction to foreigners ... Thus the question of extraterritoriality caused no difficulties during the first period of European intercourse with Japan."[27]

The generous attitude towards giving extraterritoriality to the Westerners was an even more striking feature in the case of China due to its sense of superiority as the centre of the East Asian world order. The Treaty of Nanjing contained three terms of inequality: negotiated tariff, consular jurisdiction, and MFN status. China, however, justified them by its traditional norm of "virtuous governance" (*tokuchi*). The terms were regarded as part of China's appeasement policy to the barbaric foreigners. In fact, the sense of ethical superiority of the Chinese emperor was reinforced by doing the favour of giving those rights to the Westerners. The exemption of foreigners from the Chinese law, therefore,

> was done not with any sense of loss of dignity or power, but in the condescending belief that the less civilized aliens could not understand the

> highly complex Chinese rule and must therefore be given a chance to learn the civilized way of life through gradual observation and slow assimilation. Needless to say, it was also an expedient device by which the Chinese officials could avoid the troublesome task of governing men of different tongues and modes of life.[28]

China did not understand that, by concluding the treaties with the West, it had become incorporated into a world order different from what it had been accustomed to. Nor did it understand that the new world order that the West brought was based on equal relations among sovereign states. In the case of China, opening of the five ports (Ganzhou, Amoi, Fuzhou, Ninpo, Shanghai) was not such an entirely new experience as in the case of Japan, since at least three of the ports, Amoi, Ninpo, and Shanghai, had already been open even before the arrival of the West in the nineteenth century. Also, in a vast continental country like China, the arrival of the West was taken rather as a local event which occurred on its southeastern shore. Since China was more used to dealing with the aliens than Japan, they tended to treat the arrival of the Westerners as one of those conflicts that had occasionally happened on the borders, even though the arrival of the West in China was in fact more violent in nature compared with the case of Japan. Even the great shock of the Opium War was rather absorbed in the traditional Chinese ethic of appeasing foreigners.

Concluded by Harris on July 29, 1858, the Japan-US Treaty of Amity and Commerce stated the extent and the method of extraterritoriality. To achieve his objective, Harris is known to have persuaded the Japanese by mentioning the examples of China invaded by the European powers with "much more-far-reaching and imperialistic" consequences than the United States[29] and by warning that Japan would do well to submit voluntarily to what it could not hope to avoid by resistance. Included in the treaty were important provisions for Japan to open new ports for trade and residence of Americans with diplomats and consular officials appointed in the treaty ports.[30] Even though it also contained the revisionary clause stating that, after July 4, 1872, the treaty could be revised at the request of either Japan or the United States, extraterritorial rights, which were conceded to cover civil as well as criminal cases in Article 6 of the consular jurisdiction, was one group of rights that would have never existed among the "civilised" powers at that time.[31] Harris was rather appalled at first to see Japan not showing any objection to extraterritorial rights and accepting without any hesitation the idea, for example, that the crimes committed by Americans in Japan would be tried in American consular courts. No sense of defeat or loss seemed to exist on the side of the Japanese leaders on this issue at that time.

The Japanese complacency was rather due to the imminent sense of danger of being colonised, however. By the time Harris came to demand commercial relations, Japan had already had a keen sense of possible attack by the West. The threat that Japan felt on hearing the news of the Opium War from Nagasaki and Ryūkyū is best illustrated by the order that the *bakufu* issued on August 28, 1842, one day before the conclusion of the Treaty of Nanjing, which they changed their policy of expelling all the foreign ships to that of supplying fuel, water, and food to them. This event indicates how shocked the *bakufu* was by the defeat of China by Great Britain. They immediately sensed that the British superiority would eventually affect Japan. The sense of threat and urgency was most keenly felt in Japan, even compared with China, which was directly affected through the war with Britain. Korea was also slow in reacting to the danger that might afflict the fundamental order that it relied on, largely due to the way information was brought through China.[32]

Introduction of the Law of Nations to Japan

According to Gong, Harris had started to instruct the Japanese on international law during this period.[33] Henry Wheaton's *Elements of International Law,* translated by an American missionary in China, William Alexander Parsons Martin, into Chinese and published in Beijing in 1864,[34] reached Japan in 1865.[35] Due to its wide circulation, the translation was constantly out of print in Japan. The Japanese leaders during this period focused a tremendous amount of energy on learning the international law. As Martin's translation was not a precise one, aimed only at giving the Chinese a general idea of international law, many Japanese compared the original text with Martin's translation, adding notes, explanations, and corrections.[36] Although Martin's text became the most standard, widely read book on international law in Japan for a long time, the Japanese quickly translated other books and articles on international law that became available. Mitsukuri Rinshō translated Theodore D. Woolsey's *Introduction to the Study of International Law* (1860) in 1873, and Fukuchi Genichirō translated Baron Charles de Martens's famous *Le guide diplomatique* (1854) in 1868, for example.[37]

These efforts continued throughout the 1870s and 1880s until Japan finally started producing its own works on international law. The sheer number of translations and studies that the Japanese undertook during this period demonstrates their seriousness and devotion in learning and adopting the international law. Traces of such an effort are difficult to find in China even though it had a longer history of concluding treaties with the European countries and must have had practical needs for learning international law. Taoka Ryōichi conducted a thorough study trying to elucidate this issue, concluding that the Chinese were not as enthusiastic as the Japanese in translating and introducing the international law. China's position and the pride that it had taken as the centre of East Asia can explain its slowness in reacting to the European international law and the absence of efforts to cultivate the field that Martin had opened up for them.[38]

Although Wheaton's international law took an eclectic position with regard to the source of law, drawing both on natural law and positive law, Martin's Chinese translation tended to emphasise the natural law aspect of the original text.[39] This became apparent in the efforts that Japanese translators made in comparing Wheaton's original with Martin's Chinese version. Martin is said to have edited Wheaton's text so it would suit China's ideological and social background and his missionary objective.

> In introducing international law to China, Martin was acting on the conviction that he was giving the best fruit of Christian civilization to the Chinese, and that through this work the Chinese government might be brought closer to Christianity. He wrote of it, to his friend Walter Lowrie on October 1, 1863, as 'a work which might bring this atheistic government to the recognition of God and His Eternal Justice; and perhaps impart to them something of the Spirit of Christianity.'[40]

There may have also been, however, some reluctance on the part of Martin in revealing the basis of Western domination of the world implied in international law. While the British minister in Beijing praised his work as something that "would do good by showing the Chinese that the nations of the West have principles by which they are guided, and that force is not their only law," others feared that the Chinese might use Western methods to repulse the West.[41] When Martin's Chinese translation of *Elements of International Law* first appeared, therefore, a French chargé d'affaires residing in China strongly protested

Martin's exposing the ugly side of European international law, saying that serious problems would eventually arise as a consequence.[42] In Chapter 4 of the *Elements of International Law,* Wheaton explicitly justifies the acquisition of the newly discovered lands of barbaric America, Africa, and Asia by conquest. The Westerners rather tended to keep this dark side of international law as unobtrusive as possible to states belonging outside "civilised" Europe at that time.

Another important work on international law was Nishi Shūsuke's (later Nishi Amane) *Vissering's Explanation of the Law of Nations,* published in 1868.[43] Unlike Martin's translation, Nishi's work introduced the positive international law that he had learned from the Dutch scholar Vissering, which was more standard in Europe then, with careful wording and precision. Taoka Ryōichi thought highly of Nishi's achievement and elaborated on how much care Nishi took in choosing appropriate Japanese words in his efforts to transmit the exact nuance of the lectures that he received during his two-year stay in the Netherlands.[44] Nishi was in fact the first Japanese trained in European international law and had recognised that positivism took over natural law in Europe, making a clear distinction between the two. By contrasting positive international law with natural law, Nishi contributed to introducing the essence of reality of European international law of the time to the Japanese. Implied in the positivist reality of the European international law was the "standard of civilisation," which was to define the status and the qualification of the non-European states to enter international society. While China relied heavily on naturalist understanding of international law, European positivism was, thus, more accurately brought to Japan.

The English "international law" was first translated as "*bankoku kōhō,*" which literally means "law of ten thousand nations."[45] With its naturalist nuances and universalistic appeal, it was used by the early students of international law in Japan. Mitsukuri Rinshō, who also introduced the positive international law of T. Woolsey, however, used the word "*kokusaihō,*" which carries the more exact nuance of interstate law, for the first time. This simple usage of the word "*kokusaihō*" reveals his deep understanding of European international law based on positivism. Although Mitsukuri translated the original work faithfully, he worked only on the part that dealt with the rights of sovereign independent states and the rule of non-interference. He concentrated on the parts that would relate to Japan's future revision of unequal treaties with the West and the development of domestic law systems. The practical application of international law for the negotiations and exchanges with the West was what concerned the Japanese leaders most at that time, accelerating their learning process further.[46]

Another characteristic of Japan's introduction of international law was its focus on the laws of war, which proceeded in parallel with the efforts to absorb the military knowledge of the West. One of the foremost concerns for Japan was to maintain neutrality and independence in the colonial wars that imperialist powers were conducting. At the time of the Franco-Prussian War in 1870, Japan declared neutrality at the request of France. Japan managed to submit the declaration of neutrality by somehow referring to Martin's translation but without truly understanding what it was.[47] As the Japanese learned international law out of the necessity of managing foreign relations, they restudied and retranslated the previous works of international law whenever practical needs arose, rendering the gradual Japanese understanding of laws of war close to the original and based on positivism. Martin's naturalist understanding of international law eventually disappeared as more and more Japanese engaged in the study of international law.[48]

Japanese leaders, thus, had gained knowledge of Wheaton's *Elements of International Law* and understood the gist of international law during early encounters with the West. As faithful students of international law, they displayed an unusual degree of seriousness in observing the rule of *pacta sunt servanda* (concluded treaties must be observed) in every aspect of their external behaviour. Sakamoto Ryōma, a lower-class samurai from Tosa domain who was to contribute greatly in establishing the foundations of a newly built Meiji Japan, believed that, unless Japan showed that it was behaving according to international law, the West would continue to look down on Japan as barbaric and not as an equal partner. The famous episode on his efforts to settle the case where the ship *Iroha-maru* sank due to the fault of the *bakufu* provides an example of solving the problem according to the international standard.[49] International law was to him a must in dealing with the West once a new government was established. While showing sensitivity towards how Japan might look in the eyes of other countries, the Japanese leaders represented by Sakamoto believed that Western knowledge, including international law, was something that would replace the *sword* in fighting to achieve Japan's national objectives. Leaders such as Kido Takayoshi and Iwakura Tomomi, who were to become key figures in directing Japan's foreign policy in the 1870s, also understood international law from the early period as an instrument for the strong to dominate the weak. They accepted the discrimination of the Western international society against the "uncivilised" and the "semi-civilised" embodied in international law as a reality of international life and eventually tried to apply that reality in managing relations with other Asian countries, as we will see in the next chapters. They eventually became strong advocates of the national slogan of *"fukoku kyōhei"* or "rich nation, strong army."

Conclusion

The first phase of Japan's entry into international society proved relatively smooth in the sense that Japan was not colonised and managed to maintain its independence. Two factors stand out that made Japan's encounter with the West amenable to the necessary adjustment. First was the physical preparedness of Japan, which had gradually started to modernise itself since centuries before and was equipped with advanced social infrastructures. Japan had already possessed domestic institutions that was sufficiently able to meet the Western demands when the West came: the extensive network of communication and transportation that enabled the fast delivery of information on the Western threat throughout Japan; accurate knowledge of the outside world; a strong sense of national unity and "public sphere"[50] nurtured during the era of seclusion; a large, educated population; and a market economy that substantially relied on money markets. They were "functional equivalents," culturally different from the West, but similar in institutional mechanisms. They only had to be reorganised or modified so they would fit the Western mould.[51] If the "standard of civilisation" entailed the level of development in domestic institutions, therefore, Japan had already passed the large part of the test of the standard.

The question of why only Japan in Asia had possessed social infrastructures congenial to a high level of modernisation since early times is beyond the scope of this study. Unlike the conventional view that Japan's modernisation started in Meiji with the arrival of the West, however, it has become a consensus among contemporary scholars of Japanese history that Japan's modernisation had started long before Meiji and that its level of development had competed well with the West.[52]

The second factor that facilitated Japan's adjustment in meeting the Western challenge was the leaders' realistic perceptions in directing the future course for Japan, which created and crafted consistency between Japan's domestic logic and the external demand. If an essential part of realism is the ability to achieve long-term objectives by constant consultation with the available means, Japanese political leaders were truly acting on it during this period. Determined not to follow the fate of China and India, they avoided the unnecessary internal rivalry between domains and tried to unite the country so that the West would not take advantage of the chance to intervene and colonise the country. This movement towards national unity succeeded just in time before the foreign powers were to take advantage of the unstable *bakufu*.

Externally, they tried to avoid war with the West by acceding to the unequal treaties. Opening up the country was a compromise that Japan had to make in the face of the strong West. It was based on the assessment of the country's inability to resist foreign pressure. After it had been decided that opening up the country was its course, the objective gradually shifted to the achievement of first-rank status along with the European powers. The movement to expel foreigners (*jōi*) continued, but in a different form. After Meiji, it turned into a long-term, political effort to increase Japan's national capability to fight back against the West in the future, not a short-term emotional hatred towards foreigners.

Jansen notes that, while the official restoration history emphasises Shinto purity and imperial reverence, the Japanese leaders' conduct was

> based on practical considerations and judgments. Total loyalism and complete ideological purity were luxuries that those with experience and responsibility could seldom maintain ... [It] is striking to note how seldom Sakamoto Ryōma, for example, articulated sentiments of belief in Shinto. For him the restoration of imperial rule was indeed a precondition of effective national unity,... It is perhaps this sense of individual purpose and daring, expressed in a period of national crisis, that most distinguished the Restoration heroes from so much of earlier Japanese and Chinese history.[53]

The first step and the challenge for Japan as a newcomer to the Western system was how to survive as an independent state. After Japan's direction was generally set on building a modern nation centring around the emperor with equal relations with other powers, it started to vigourously learn about the West. By the time of the Meiji Restoration, the "standard of civilisation" often considered as imposed by the West gradually changed into something that was to be positively absorbed and adapted by Japan. "What began as outrage against intrusive foreigners had become anger directed at a polity that did not conform to international standards."[54]

While the actual Western threat was not as great as often perceived, Japan responded to it quickly. This was due to two factors. First, with the development of the domestic information-delivering network during the Edo period, the Japanese national had relatively easy access to information. The fact that Japan was exposed to foreign influence during the sixteenth century before the isolationist policy came into effect in the early seventeenth century also had nurtured Japan's sensitivity to the Western threat. Restricted amounts of information that had been brought from the *dejima*[55] in Nagasaki during the seclusion period further encouraged keen attention on the part of the Japanese to external events. Second, the leaders exaggerated the threat and used it in uniting the country, convincing the public to bear the cost, resulting in a peaceful ending of the Tokugawa regime by avoiding significant civil wars. The moderate nature of the encounter with the West saved Japan energy for socialisation.

Japanese leaders in particular demonstrated a strong proclivity to learning positivist international law prevalent during this period. In adopting international law, they saw utility in transforming the national energy to building a modern nation, revising unequal treaties, and eventually changing and organising the power relations of East Asia. Establishment of constitutional government with representative institutions was considered as the foremost item on the agenda, since it was the best way to imprint Japan's progress on the West.

The introduction of international law in Japan was remarkably energetic, with many translations of various works on international law becoming available while Japan was in the middle of domestic turmoil from overthrowing the *bakufu* and introducing the new Meiji government. We have seen that Japan's adoption of the Law of Nations was characterised by its faithfulness to the original text, its accurate grasp of the essence of positivism, and its focus on the law of war. The adoption of positivist international law, which had taken the place of natural law, starting with Moser and Martens in the late eighteenth century,[56] owes much to Nishi, who introduced Visserling's private lectures for himself and his colleague Tsuda with an amazing precision. The leaders demonstrated a high degree of understanding that came close to the essence of international law in an extremely short period of time, even though most of them did not have any academic training in international law.

Due to the many treaties that needed to be concluded and negotiations to be conducted, the Japanese adoption of international law was based on the practical needs of dealing with the international law. From the time of its adoption, therefore, international law for Japan was something for immediate use.

4 Absorption: "Civilisation and Enlightenment," 1870s

This chapter investigates how Japan absorbed Western civilisation and international law by focusing on a mission that the Japanese government sent abroad to study the essence of Western society and civilisation and on several negotiations that Japan conducted with other countries. The eagerness to learn and abide by international law and to demonstrate their will and capacity to become a faithful adherent of it was most manifested in the way political leaders interacted with other Asian and Western countries during this era.

The Japanese Foreign Ministry was established in 1869 with Sawa Nobuyoshi appointed as the first foreign minister (then called *gaimukyō*). The dates for the negotiations on treaty revision with the Western powers were approaching.[1] One year prior to these dates, Sawa notified the Western powers of Japan's desire for revision. After Sawa, Iwakura Tomomi (1825–83), a court noble with a keen sense of foreign threat who was also a strong supporter of the early revision of the unequal treaties, took over the position in July 1871.

Often called a founding father of Japanese foreign policy, Iwakura as a personality with his complex character and policy ideas invites careful investigation. Keen on the reality of power politics among nations, he was sceptical of the superficial equality among nations from early on and regarded international law as a tool of the strong. In his memorandum on treaty revision of February 1869, Iwakura said:

> We must revise the treaties of commerce and navigation already concluded with Britain, France, Prussia and the United States and thus protect the independence of our country. Consular jurisdiction cannot be tolerated. If foreigners unreasonably refuse to revise their treaties, we must argue with

> them on the basis of reason. Foreigners have the spirit of the tiger and the wolf; and, if we are afraid of their tyranny, our country will become their slave. Whenever Japanese and foreigners have been involved in fights with one another, it was only Japanese who killed foreigners that have in the past been required to pay compensation and not the foreigners. The emperor's honor is thereby impaired; national rights are restricted; this is intolerable to us. We must devise laws to govern relations with foreign countries. If any clash takes place between Japanese and foreigners from now on, we should resolve it by these laws.[2]

Acknowledging Iwakura's deep resentment against unequal treaties, Ian Nish characterises his political style as prudent and moderate in achieving his objectives and negotiating the abrogation of unequal treaties. Iwakura was a political figure who never sacrificed his long-term goals for the pursuit of short-term goals. In his efforts to build a new political edifice that would take over the *bakufu,* he above all avoided radical measures that might invite domestic unrest and insurgency, and considered the increase in Japan's national power as the country's formost goal in order to live through the international reality of the survival of the fittest.[3]

Although he was an official of the court of the emperor, Iwakura never joined the radical anti-shogun movement. He was careful not to incite civil war in Japan, which would encourage foreign intervention and colonisation. During his extremely short service in the Foreign Ministry between 1869 and 1871 before he was appointed as the Minister of the Right in October 1871, he was determined to remain discreet and cautious in directing Japan's future course.

The Iwakura Mission, 1871–3

The Iwakura Mission, a delegation that was originally created to negotiate treaty revision as its foremost objective, visited nine cities in the United States and twelve countries in Europe over a period of almost two years. It was one of the events by which Iwakura's reputation as a balanced, farsighted foreign policy expert soared. Iwakura, envoy extraordinary ambassador plenipotentiary, influenced all aspects of the mission, including the objective, the composition, and the itinerary.[4] The importance placed on the mission can be easily understood by its size and by the fact that almost all prominent young Japanese statesmen participated in it, virtually emptying the Japanese government for two years, with important national issues to be deferred until their return. Among the members of the group were Kido Takayoshi, Ōkubo Toshimichi, Itō Hirobumi, and Mori Arinori, for example, who became the central figures of the new Meiji government established in 1868. As is well known, it had three major objectives: first, to negotiate revision of unequal treaties; second, to observe, investigate, and learn from other advanced countries for the purposes of domestic reform; and third, to enhance friendship among nations.

The mission's foremost objective of negotiating the treaty revisions met with difficulties from the start. The drafts for the revision that the mission prepared in the first negotiations with US statesmen requested tariff autonomy and abrogation of extraterritoriality upon the establishment of Japanese domestic laws based on the laws in the United States and European countries. They were, however, flatly rejected during the first days of the mission, as US officials perceived the domestic conditions in Japan as too immature[5] and were adamant that the unequal treaties would not be negotiated until Japan could demonstrate a system of adequate jurisprudence.

Itō and Ōkubo, the two deputy leaders of the mission, also had to return to Japan in order to obtain plenipotentiary authority for Iwakura on request of the American Secretary of State, Hamilton Fish. It became an embarrassing anecdote that demonstrates the ignorance of the Japanese political leaders about a basic international custom that a good student of international law should have known. It took almost four months for Itō and Ōkubo to go back to Japan to obtain the authority and return to Washington, D.C. When the discussions on treaty revision were nonetheless broken off after all this hustle, disappointing many, Iwakura decided to avoid formal negotiations and to hold informal conversations with the statesmen of the treaty powers, only letting them know the intention of Japan's desire for early revision. The conversations on negotiating treaty reforms remained exploratory in Europe, too, with the issue to be further examined on their return to Japan.

The significance of the Iwakura Mission, therefore, did not lie in achieving anything tangible in negotiating the revision, but in affecting the perceptions of the Japanese leaders concerning international politics and on how Japan should act in order to enter the European club of international society. On the second objective of the mission, "to observe, investigate, and learn from other advanced countries," Kume Kunitake left fascinating records of the mission members' observations in the United States and Europe.[6] The Japanese leaders came to clearly understand the Japan's status and level of development in light of the requirements placed on a state as a modern, civilised nation, what they needed to do to join the great powers, and how they should achieve that objective. When the mission visited the United States and Europe, the Western countries were experiencing a golden age of peace and industrial development. The mission made close observations of every aspect of Western civilisation and selected what to adopt from which country for Japan's modern nation building, which would eventually lead to full membership in international society. Japan was most influenced by the United States as to the content of education, for example, while the educational system itself was copied from France.

Although the leaders did observe Western superiority over Japan, they also came to learn that this was only a recent phenomenon and that Japan was not as far behind as they had thought. Aside from Britain, which had already been thriving for centuries, most of the Western countries had achieved rapid economic growth in just three decades or so. The Japanese leaders saw that even recently formed countries such as Prussia could raise national prestige by using international law tactically to its advantage and achieve equal status with the great powers in international society. On March 15, 1872, Japanese leaders visiting Prussia listened to Otto von Bismarck's speech on the hypocrisy of international law and learned that the realm of international politics is that of the law of the jungle. According to Kume's records, Bismarck said:

> It is said that every country interacts with other states on the basis of friendship, harmony, and protocol. However, this is merely superficial lip-service, behind which lies actual practice; the insults to which the strong subject the weak, and the scorn the big hold for the little. When I was a child, our Prussia was poor and weak, as I am sure Your Excellencies all know. At that time, I summarized for myself the histories of small countries, and the anger with which I burned then remains clearly in my memory. [I perceived that] the so-called law of all countries argued to the profit of the great nations. If it had any profit in it for them, the powerful would apply the law of nations to the letter, but when it lacked attractions, the law of nations was jettisoned, and military might employed, irregardless of convention. The small nations diligently consulted precedent and justification. Nevertheless, although they believed that if they did not cross any boundaries their sovereign rights would be defended, their governments were frittered away by foreign insults and contempt, leading,

> in almost every case, to an inability to preserve their independence. This happened all the time. I was consumed by resentment.
>
> I considered that once a country increases its power, it becomes a nation that has to be treated as an equal by other states. Patriotism spurred me from the age of ten years to achieve my wish, which was, in short, nothing more than a desire to defend our sovereign rights against all states ... in European diplomacy, trust alone is not yet sufficient. I believe I am right in saying that Your Excellencies also do not give free rein to negligence.[7]

Bismarck further stated that the objective of his diplomacy lay in establishing equal diplomatic relations and that Britain and France were exploiting overseas colonies to the regret of all the other countries.[8] From his speech, the leaders came to understand the great gap that existed between the ideal of international law, which is equality among nations, and the reality of international politics, where power considerations dominate. The Iwakura Mission, thus, also marked a turning point in the Japanese perception and interpretation of international law. While the overall *Zeitgeist* of the era during this period was "civilisation and enlightenment," the Japanese leaders were introduced to the negative aspects of international law; that is, actual inequality among nations in the guise of international law.

The Iwakura Mission functioned as a measurement of Japan not only against the West, but also against Asian countries, China in particular, in the degree of modernisation and civilisation.[9] It gave the Japanese leaders a sense of confidence that their country was faring better than other Asian countries. Since Japan had long been concerned with the situation in China, which became prey for the West, their recognition that their country had managed relations with the West better than China had led them to dissociate Japan from other Asian countries with increased confidence about joining the West.

After his return to Japan, Iwakura continued to influence Japanese foreign policy behind the scenes, especially after Ōkubo was assassinated in 1878. He ascended to the top of foreign affairs, where he stayed until his death in 1883. Japan's realistic, pragmatic foreign policy behaviour in the 1870s owes much to Iwakura. The cautious temperament required for statesmanship was an attitude that leaders in the Iwakura Mission learned to adopt in the course of their two-year travels. They continued to display this attitude in managing relations with foreign powers after returning from the mission, whether in settling territorial questions with Russia, in deciding on the treatment of Korea, or in the so-called Taiwan Expedition, as will be discussed in the next section of this chapter. As their cautious approach to foreign affairs contradicted the radical domestic proponents for foreign expeditions, all the leaders exposed to the knowledge about the situations in the West argued against Japan's potential adventurism in its policy towards Korea, which they had to face on their return from the mission.[10] They believed that the country should be focusing on developing effective domestic organisations, especially legal systems, instead of dispatching troops abroad. The advocates of an expedition to Korea were eventually contained by the participants of the Iwakura Mission.

On the mission's return, Japan energised itself in building a modern nation-state with the slogan of "rich state, strong army" (*fukoku kyōhei*) and "increase production and promote industry" (*shokusan kogyō*) under Minister of Internal Affairs Ōkubo's leadership.[11] The political leaders strongly felt the need to reform some domestic institutions including a parliamentary system, public participation, and legal systems, before European powers would entertain renegotiations. While Japan had focused on developing a modern military in the 1850s and 1860s, it also started to further modernise the nation in other aspects of political and social life to obtain international prestige and respect.[12] It was in the 1870s, for example, when Western styles of tax, postal, and monetary systems were established. Bringing the domestic legal system into line with the prevalent European ones was one of the agenda items that Japan had been facing since the 1860s. As the Europeans demanded that the life, liberty, and property of their nationals be guaranteed if the extraterritorial systems were to be lifted, Japan had examined the civil and criminal codes of numerous countries in the course of reforming its legal systems. These efforts bore fruit in the 1880s and 1890s with the promulgation of a constitution and the enactment of criminal and civil codes. These administrative and legal reforms paralleled introduction of all aspects of Western culture.

Accommodation to the Western Norm: A New Style of Japanese Diplomacy

During this period, a notable change occurred in Japan's style of diplomacy in handling international issues involving its neighbours. The change in Japanese attitudes towards the Eurocentric international norms can be most clearly observed in its diplomatic relations with other Asian countries in the 1870s, when Japan applied several lessons that it had learned since the 1850s through its intercourse with the European powers.

In negotiating treaties with Korea and China, Japan consciously tried to employ Western legal concepts and used English. Alexis Dudden claims that the Meiji government tried to change the power configuration of Asia by speaking English in those negotiations.[13] While Japan had traditionally complied with the Chinese diplomatic style in negotiating with Asian countries, Western legal concepts and terms turned out to provide useful guidance in directing negotiations to the advantage of Japan, denying the traditional Chinese leadership in diplomacy.

The Taiwan Incident

The Taiwan Incident, or Formosan Expedition in 1874, became one of the early cases in which Japan settled an international dispute by using the Western vocabulary of international law. One of the foci of contention between China and Japan in the Taiwan Incident was over the jurisdiction and diplomatic position of Ryūkyū (present Okinawa Prefecture), where the Satsuma domain had been exercising its control. Japan had had a garrison there since the end of the Edo Period and had declared its jurisdiction over it on October 16, 1872.[14] China, however, had never admitted Japan's sovereignty over the Ryūkyū Islands. The incident occurred when a Ryūkyūan ship was stranded off the eastern coast of Taiwan in December 1871. Fifty-four out of the sixty-six Ryūkyūans on board were murdered in a cruel manner by the Formosan aborigines. Consequently, the Ryūkyū government complained to the Japanese government.

By this time, Japan was well aware of the Western style of settling this kind of matter and considered the incident as a perfect opportunity to make the case an instance of applying the Western style of international settlement that it had been learning. A similar incident, in fact, had occurred with a wrecked American ship, the *Rover*, in 1867, where all the Americans on board were killed by Taiwanese aborigines. In this incident, China claimed that eastern Taiwan was "not under its jurisdiction" (*kegai*) and refused to take responsibility. The United States settled the incident by sending a punitive expedition and discussing the matter with the aboriginal chiefs.[15] Following this example, Japan first decided to try negotiating with China with the possibility of sending an expedition in case China refused to take responsibility.

As expected, China insisted that it had no responsibility for the murders because the eastern coast of Taiwan was not under Chinese jurisdiction. China's denial of its sovereignty over Taiwan justified the Meiji government's sending of a punitive expedition. China protested vigourously against the expedition, stating that "the eastern portion of Formosa was an integral part of the Chinese Empire and that Japan had invaded Chinese territory, not only without her approval, but against her protests."[16] At this point, Ōkubo Toshimichi, famous for his elegant forensic style, was appointed as minister plenipotentiary and went to Beijing in September 1874 for negotiations. He is said to have prepared for the coming negotiations on the way to China by debating international law with Gustave E. Boissonade, one of the legal advisors employed by the Meiji government, who was on the ship.[17] Ōkubo's diary records a considerable amount of counselling that he received from Boissonade.[18]

When he reached China, Ōkubo mentioned that China had initially denied that it had jurisdiction over Taiwan, which meant Taiwan was a barbarian no-man's land from the point-of-view of international law. In the actual negotiation with the *Zonli Yamen*,[19] Ōkubo accused China of not dispatching troops nor setting up an administration on the southern part of Taiwan while claiming its jurisdiction. Basing his claim on the positivist international law, he stated: "By the law of nations, newly discovered land belongs to whoever first exercises real power over it, builds an administrative center on it, and undertakes the actual management of its affairs."[20] He had also prepared another accusation that could be raised against China in case China insisted on its sovereignty over Taiwan: Why didn't China take the full responsibility in protecting foreigners in accordance with international law, if Taiwan belonged to China?

China continued to be evasive and vague, insisting on settling matters not by Western international law but by their concept of justice and reason. Japan was tactically in an advantageous position here, since, if China denied its sovereignty over Taiwan, it should have no protest against Japan's protecting its citizens; if China claimed sovereignty, it failed to take responsibility for the massacred Ryūkyūans. When the negotiation was finally about to be settled by the arbitration of British minister Thomas Wade, Ōkubo requested that written promises, not verbal ones, be made. He demanded that China recognise the Japanese expedition as a "just attempt to protect its own subjects" (*homin no gikyo*) and that China pay 500,000 taels[21] as proposed by China itself and conveyed by Wade. A treaty was signed on October 31, 1874, with the acknowledgement of Japanese sovereignty over the Ryūkyūs, indemnity of China, and withdrawal of the Japanese forces from Taiwan.[22]

While the expedition cost more than Japan received from China as indemnity, the significance lay in making China recognise Japan's sovereignty over Ryūkyū and in demonstrating to the world the use of Western international law in settling disputes in East Asia. In the Taiwan Incident, Japan insisted that a conflict be settled based on international law. Ōkubo used international law as an ethical standard to persuade China and to gain support from the West. Stern states that "Ōkubo felt that Japan was to be the diplomatic leader in Asia based on its superior understanding of the changing diplomatic situation in the East … Ōkubo was making sure that he would have the ability to make Japan the leader of Asian diplomacy in a way that would not alarm the West, but that would not rely on it either."[23] The traditional cultural tie between Japan and China was taken over by an objective diplomatic standard of exchange. In 1885 Taiwan Province was established by China. By establishing friendly relations with the Western diplomatic community while maintaining relations with China and uniting Asia under the modern leadership of Japan, Ōkubo successfully manipulated international law.[24]

The Kanghwa Incident

The Kanghwa Incident in 1875 and Kanghwa Treaty in 1876 were important steps in the Japanese application of international law and exercise of leadership in Asia. They also represented another change in Japan's stance in Asia and in the world. The incident occurred when Koreans attacked a Japanese battleship in September 1875 in the coastal waters near Korea, offending Japan. In its efforts to settle the problem by international law, Japan tried to persuade Korea, a protectorate of China comfortably maintaining its status within a Confucian framework of interstate relations, to end its isolation policy, proposing to recognise Korea as an independent state. Korea, however, kept declining Japan's persistent requests for exchanges between the two "equal" countries.

Korea had disdained Japan for two reasons. First, as a faithful participant in the *Ka-I* (China and barbaric others) system, Korea was worried about China's reaction to Japan's overtures for equal relations with Korea as two sovereign states. Second was the personal distaste of the Korean ruler, Tai-in-kun, for Japan's radical changes once the country opened up, including: wearing Western clothes and hairstyle, building railroads, and trying to catch up with European industrial standards, all of which he considered undignified. In the eyes of Korea, it was the West that was backward and barbaric and yet the Japanese were now implying that it was Asia that was barbaric. On the part of Japan, its rationale for identifying Korea as an independent state was based on international law, as the Meiji government had repeatedly emphasised since the Restoration.

In March 1873, Foreign Minister Soejima Taneomi visited Beijing to discuss Korea's unruly attitude, as exemplified by a sign posted at a public house earlier that year that called Japan a "country of no law." Soejima's hope was that China would give Japan freedom of action to send a military expedition to the peninsula. China, however, rejected his request. The Japanese were divided between those favouring punishment for Korea (*seikanron*) and those opposed to it. Political leaders such as Iwakura and others who were on the Iwakura Mission thought that Japan should wait to take a punitive line until Japan's wealth and power reached the standards of great powers. The propunishment group eventually lost. Japan would use force in the worst case, but meanwhile would negotiate by nonmilitary means.[25] Korea did not seem to want the matter to escalate into war, either.

As Korea started to show more congenial attitudes by gradually conceding to the Japanese objections, the Treaty of Commerce and Friendship (Treaty of Kanghwa) was finally signed in 1876, opening three Korean ports to Japanese trade and securing consular jurisdiction and tariff immunity. The treaty turned out to be similar in content to the first two treaties that Japan signed with the United States. In persuading Korea, Japan applied the same technique and excuse that Perry used in entering Edo Bay in 1854: "A combination of gunboat diplomacy in the interests of 'free trade imperialism.'"[26] Thus, Korea was placed in a status similar to that of Japan in the earlier period.[27] By confirming control over Korea with a legal rationale, Japan also tried to impress other countries as the leader of Asia. This declaration of Korean independence denied its tributary status, humiliating China similarly to the way the Taiwan Incident was settled.

Border Problems with Russia

Still another example of Japan's application of international law in actual negotiations was the border issue over Sakhalin Island, which had been a source of troubles between Japan and Russia for more than a century. Japan and Russia signed the Treaty of Peace and Amity in 1855 (Treaty of Shimoda), which recognised Russian jurisdiction over the Kurile Islands and Japanese jurisdiction over the islands south of

Eterup. Both Japanese and Russians continued to live in Sakhalin, however, leaving its jurisdiction vague. By the 1870s the border issue over Sakhalin Island had become stormy as both countries asserted their rights and attempted to colonise it. The Russians sent emigrants in an attempt to establish a *de facto* government there. Starting in the late 1850s, Japan had sent envoys to St. Petersburg several times, proposing to divide the island at the fiftieth parallel. After learning from the United States that it had bought Alaska from Russia, Soejima, the then state councillor, proposed purchasing the north of Sakhalin Island for 2,000,000 yen. After Russia refused the offer, Japan negotiated the acquisition of all of Kurile Islands, including Urup, Kunashiri, and Eterup, in exchange for all of Sakhalin Island.

On May 7, 1875, a treaty to exchange Sakhalin Island with the Kurile Islands was concluded. The treaty granted to "Japanese ships entering the port of Kirsakov exemption from the customs tariffs and harbor duties for ten years and the right of appointing the Japanese Consul there, and to Japanese vessels and merchants of the most favoured nations in regard to fishing and navigation in the Okhotsk Sea and along the coast of Kamtchatka."[28] Giving up all of Sakhalin Island in exchange for the central and northern Kurile Islands enabled Japan to retain important mining and fishing resources. Considering the power gap between Russia and Japan in terms of the size of arms and population at this time, this was not a bad deal for Japan. Japan needed to refrain from radical behaviour on a sensitive border issue often tied to nationalism of a newly developed state, which tends to excite and agitate the public. The conciliatory line towards the Russians to avoid future rivalry was an indication of Japan's realism and prudence in diplomacy that was salient during this period. Not only was what Japan gained in the treaty quite reasonable in itself, but also the negotiations were conducted on an equal basis, which had great symbolic meanings for Japan in its struggle for full-fledged membership in the international community.

In 1876, Japan also consolidated its sovereignty over the Ogasawara Islands (Bonin Islands), which turned out to be a much easier process than the case of Sakhalin Island due to the voluntary renouncement of the United States. The border on the East was thus defined along with Taiwan and Kamtchatka.

Conclusion

The 1870s was an era of Japan's naïve admiration and adoration for the "civilised" West. In parallel with the drastic changes in the domestic political system from a feudal polity to the Meiji government in 1868, absorption of the norm of international society proceeded at a rapid pace. Where the new era required new purposes and directions for Japan, "civilisation and enlightenment" filled the void. An international rationale worked for Japan's domestic reforms, while a domestic rationale necessitated Japan's improved external relations.

The Iwakura Mission affected the conduct of Japanese foreign policy in this period in three ways. First, it eliminated the possibility of extremist moves on the part of Japan and fostered prudent attitudes among leaders in pursuing its national objective. It was critically important for leaders to check and contain radical national movements in the era of great transformation, as many modern ideas on people's rights started to be introduced domestically. Second, it gave Japan a strong incentive for nation building based on the Western model. The leaders learned to understand precisely what Japan needed to do both domestically and internationally for the treaty revision. Third, it convinced Japan of its strong potential to be qualified as a member of European international society. The leaders of the mission were especially encouraged by the Prussian model of nation building.

Japan started to demonstrate its clear desire and capacity to accommodate the Western logic embodied in international law for upgrading its international position in Asia, which would eventually give Japan membership in Eurodominant international society. Afraid of being looked down on as an uncivilised country and desiring early amendment of the unequal treaties, Japan started to display an unusual degree of adherence and care in observing international law during this period of its ascendance. Perhaps no country was more faithful to and eager to absorb the norms of international society than Japan was during this period. In military colleges, for example, a great amount of time was spent in instructing students in international law. This eagerness eventually came to bear fruit in Japan's observant conduct during the Sino-Japanese War, the Boxer Rebellion, and the Russo-Japanese War.

While China was still claiming its traditional suzerainty over Korea, Japan continued to appeal to the international community for the lawfulness of its foreign conduct. The political leaders strongly believed that observance of international law and living up to international credentials were critical components of the "civilisation" required for membership in international society. As the government also undertook treaties to justify its colonial policies by following the international standard embodied in international law, the concept of international law gradually became the concept of power in East Asia.

Japan's compliance with positivist Western norms, which was considered a must for national survival and independence in the earlier period, eventually became something that Japan was eager to embrace, especially after it gained more confidence about its national capability and status. By the end of the 1870s, Japanese leaders felt that their country had coped with the hardest trial by avoiding colonisation and that it was dealing with Western countries better than other Asian countries. While the leaders may have continued to emphasise threat and foreign pressure, the threat was rather used to unite and urge the country towards further national development.[29] It was no longer such a critical concern as to threaten Japan's survival as an independent state. The driving force for Japan was the confidence that Japanese leaders had obtained through their contact with the West in the early 1870s as well as their concomitant fascination with Western civilisation. When survival ceased to be an issue, Japan concentrated on nation building, assimilating the Western civilisation wholeheartedly.

The 1870s marked the emergence of new domestic institutions of a modern centralised state that had enormous impacts on Japanese society: abolition of feudal domains (1871), the Education Order (1872), Land Tax Reform (1873), and Military Conscription Ordinance (1873), to name a few. In parallel with the establishment of these institutions one after another, the Meiji government employed thousands of foreign advisers, instructors, and educators (*oyatoi gaikoku-jin*) to help with modernisation and civilisation.[30] The daily life of ordinary people was also dramatically changed during this period, with the ordinance to cut off the topknots (*danpatsurei,* 1871), establishment of postal service (1871) and railways (1872), adoption of the Gregorian calendar (1873), and an ordinance to prohibit wearing swords (1876), for example. Gong notes:

> By 1873, soaps, watches, gold chains, umbrellas, Western hats, jackets, trousers, and shoes were the veneer of an adoration of things Western that went deeper to include Western literature, philosophies, politics, religion, architecture, painting, sculpture, and music. By 1875, gas lamps flickered at the Imperial Palace gates and the first brick building had been erected on the Ginza. In short, the changes in Japan's political organization, and in its diplomatic and legal sectors, were part of a much larger movement to emulate the general civilization of the West. A consequence of Japan's acceptance of European standards of "civilization" was the Japanese recognition that they were "uncivilized" and "backward." Emphasising the universal, scientific nature of "civilization" in general did not belie the fact

> that to embrace the ideas, institutions, and material symbols of European civilization meant to 'move away from tradition, to relegate some of its inherited ideas and institutions to history, usually with some dismissive phrase describing them as "old fashioned" or "out of date."[31]

Japan obtained substantial control over tariff and trade regulations in the treaty between Japan and the United States in July 1878,[32] while the acquisition of equal status in diplomacy remained an unsolved item on the agenda for the Meiji government. By the 1880s, the Western powers were seeking colonies in every corner of the globe, making the issues of lifting extraterritoriality and regaining tariff control ever more pressing for Japan so it would not be late for colonial competition. In 1888, Japan succeeded in signing a treaty with Mexico based on complete equality between states for the first time. The European powers, however, were not ready to shed their extraterritorial privileges, which provided them with rights and protection. While Japan's objective of joining the civilised members of international society had become clear, they still took a united front in maintaining these advantages.[33]

Japan was to reach the final stage of its efforts to revise the unequal treaty in the 1890s, when it engaged in actual negotiations with the West both inside and outside of Japan. The skillful tactics of negotiation finally bore fruit in 1899 in the form of abrogation of extraterritoriality, whose process I will now track in the next chapter.

5 Adaptation: International Law as a Tool, 1880s–90s

By 1880 Japan had separated itself from the rest of Asia. Having learned that the source of energy for the West's expansion was imperialism and colonialism, it started to apply what it had experienced as a subordinate to Western superiority to its relations with other Asian countries. After the deaths of Kido and Saigō in 1877 and the assassination of Ōkubo in 1878, perceptions of Japanese political leaders about the nation's role in East Asia dramatically changed. Until around the 1880s, their objective was to cooperate with China and guide other countries as the Asian leader in order to eventually counter the West. Subsequently, however, Japan started to display its strong stance to "leave" Asia. Fukuzawa Yukichi, the foremost intellectual leader of the era who used to advocate mutual diplomatic ties with China, started to cut off Asia by the time he published his famous *An Outline of a Theory of Civilisation* in 1875. His "*Datsuaron* [Theory of Leaving Asia]" argued that, if Japan did not wish to be mixed with other underdeveloped countries, Japan must forget Asia.[1] One reason for these attitudinal changes was, first of all, that Japan was disappointed at the achievements of other Asian countries, especially China and Korea, in demonstrating willingness and capability to modernise. The possibility of forming Asian alliances, which had preoccupied the Japanese leaders' minds previously, thus failed to become a reality. Coincidentally, Darwin's theory of evolution was introduced at this time and also applied to interpret the nature of international relations. In the contest of the "survival of the fittest," Japan started to identify itself with the stronger side.

Japan's understanding of international law has matured since the initial adoption of Wheaton's text through the era of "absorption." In accordance with the change of perception among the political leaders with regard to the nature of international law and international politics in general, Japan gradually started to demonstrate a realistic understanding in its application of international law as a tool of the strong. International law became something that Japan could use not only as an agreed-upon method of protecting various interests among great powers, but also of an enhancement of national power.

We saw in Chapter 4 that the Japanese leaders started to base their external conduct on the rules of international law in dealing with disputes with neighbouring countries in Asia, taking advantage of its legitimacy as a standard source of guidance in the management of international affairs on the one hand and impressing the West with Japan's loyalty to the European code of conduct on the other. In the final stage of negotiating its qualifications for full international membership, symbolised by the lifting of extraterritoriality, Japan's efforts, skills, and tactics culminated in the act of finally convincing the European powers of the justice of revising unequal treaties. By this time Japan's faithfulness to the international law was firmly engraved in the minds of the Western powers.

This chapter will provide an overview of the final negotiation process that evolved from the era of Inoue Kaoru to the era of Mutsu Munemitsu as foreign minister. The negotiation process became increasingly complicated and delicate, as leaders needed to treat public opinion and the power game among the European powers simultaneously with extra care, in addition to the actual negotiations themselves. In the latter part of this chapter, I will outline the efforts and manoeuvres of the leaders in appealing to the West. After imprinting their faithful observance of international law on the mind of the Western powers, the strategies and manipulations of the political leaders succeeded in convincing them to abrogate extraterritoriality.

Several incidents had occurred in the late 1870s that clearly demonstrated the priority of getting the extraterritoriality issues straight. In February 1878, opium secretly imported by a British merchant, John Hartley, was brought to light. Under British consular jurisdiction, however, he was presumed innocent on the grounds that the opium poppy was a medicinal plant. Japan also faced the agony of cholera brought by the West.[2] In the cholera-infected years, so-called "cholera riots" or "cholera uprisings" repeatedly occurred, with the most severe consequences in 1877, 1879, 1882, 1885, 1886, 1890, 1891, and 1895. As the Japanese government had no right to quarantine foreign ships, however, the bacteria entered the country freely. When Foreign Minister Terajima

Munenori notified the Western powers of the regulation for quarantine in 1879, he met with strong opposition from the West – afraid of the domino effect that this might have with other countries once they followed Japanese regulations.

Another distressing affair was the Normanton Incident of October 1886, in which all the twenty-three Japanese passengers on the British ship *Normanton* were drowned while all the British crew were saved after escaping from the ship, when it sank off the shore of Kii domain. The British crew, however, were judged not guilty, enraging the Japanese. Even after the Japanese government convicted the captain of murder, the court decided only to put the captain in jail for three months for committing homicide by misadventure. No compensation was paid for the dead. As the "evil" of consular jurisdiction became obvious in the eyes of the Japanese, lifting of the unequal treaties as the root cause of the problem became a pressing issue to be addressed.

Endless Negotiations

The Era of Inoue

Inoue Kaoru became foreign minister on September 10, 1879. As the function of the foreign minister's office was clearly defined in accordance with the development of the cabinet system during the era of Inoue, the title changed from "*gaimukyō*" to "*gaimudaijin.*" Inoue was thoroughly immersed in the treaty reform issue, concentrating on legal rights (extraterritoriality) rather than tariff rights, which his predecessor had focused on. Japan needed to convince the West of treaty reform by making the West feel a sense of Japan's advancement and Westernisation.

Multilateral conferences on treaty reform were frequently held during Inoue's tenure. With the treaty revision becoming a pressing issue for Japan, thirty-six conferences on treaty reform were held in 1886. Inoue was an enthusiastic moderniser, who believed that the unequal treaties, including the law codes and access to the Japanese hinterland by foreigners,would be lifted only when Japan was sufficiently Westernised.[3] During the era of Inoue, the Westernisation process was greatly facilitated with the help of *oyatoi gaikoku-jin* employed by the government. Inoue's sense of urgency, however, made his treaty revision plan rather modest, as he made many concessions to the West in order to bring about an early revision. Inoue cautiously proposed creation of a Japanese court composed with a majority of foreign judges and to let foreigners be tried by them. When the proposal was about to be accepted by the great powers, word of it leaked, creating a storm of nationwide protest against Inoue. Viscount General Tani Tateki, the minister of the Agricultural and Commerce Department also known as Tani Kanjō, expressed strong opposition against the secret style of Inoue. Tani had never been consulted about the matter even though his Department would be greatly affected by the treaty reform.[4] Led by Tani, the antigovernment forces gained ground for objecting to the proposals to appoint Western judges for cases involving foreigners. In reply to Tani's opposition, Inoue argued on various aspects of Japanese societal infrastructure still insufficient to qualify for a civilised member of the Western club of international society and on the necessity for Japan to make concessions to the West:

> We must set up a new "civilised state" here and our countrymen must become people of knowledge and vigour by free contact with people from the West … We need to build up a European civilisation here on a par with that of civilised European states. We must inaugurate here a new-style "European empire." To this end, Japan will for the first time by treaty occupy a position equal to the European powers. For us to revise the present treaties will mark the very first step on the road to achieving this great purpose. There are certain items on which we should make concessions in negotiating for treaty revision because our present level of civilisation is lower. Of course, extraterritorial jurisdiction is harmful because of the unlawful acts of foreigners and their possessing "immovable property." But Japan's law codes are deficient; our courts are in their infancy.[5]

It was Inoue's intention to complete the treaty revision before the constitution came into effect, as the inauguration of the Diet was expected to open the floodgates of political criticism against the treaties.[6] As he continued to keep the content of the negotiations for the treaty reform secret from the public, Boissonade, a French law advisor to the Japanese government, opposed the way Inoue was handling the matter. With the aim of raising public opposition against the government over the treaty reform issue, he publicised the treaty reform drafts that were being negotiated secretly. This ended Inoue's attempt at treaty reform, postponing the conference for the reform indefinitely in July 1887.

Meanwhile, it was during the era of Inoue that Itō Hirobumi, the ambassador to China, came to conclude the Tienjing Treaty in 1885 with China to settle the coup d'etat in Seoul waged by liberal Korean leaders backed by Japan against China. Having mastered Western-style negotiation techniques during his stay in the United States and in Europe, Itō negotiated the terms of Chinese withdrawal from the Korean peninsula, referring to international law whenever the negotiations seemed to deadlock. By using the logic of the Western international system that he had just learned from the West and by using English for international legal terms,[7] he led to reorganise the power relations in East Asia by European international law, shedding the suzerain international relations predominant in the Chinese international system.

The Era of Ōkuma

Ōkuma Shigenobu took over after Inoue resigned on February 1, 1888. While Inoue tried to negotiate with treaty powers collectively, Ōkuma negotiated the revision problem on a bilateral basis, concentrating on Britain. He kept, however, the details of the negotiations under wraps as Inoue did. Ōkuma had expected that a success in concluding the equal treaty with Mexico in 1888 with provisions on commerce and navigation, trading duties, and judicial autonomy would lead to another with other countries. He could not, however, yet obtain consent from other countries on treaty revisions based on complete equality.

Ōkuma was eager to distinguish himself as a leader of external affairs as opposed to Itō Hirobumi, who had rendered meritorious service in promulgating the Constitution, the most important preoccupation of Japanese leaders at that time. While the promulgation of the Constitution would work to convince the West of Japan's qualification for a full international membership as a symbol of Japan's sufficient level of modernisation, negotiations on treaty revision had to go through vehement discussions and debates in the Diet, where forceful opposition and counterchecks were expected from different political parties.[8]

Ōkuma modified Inoue's proposal on the revision by limiting the number of foreign judges to be invited to the Supreme Court (*Daishin-in*). The Japanese public, however, was still angry at the proposal to invite foreign judges to Japanese courts. The treaty revision had become such a sensitive issue for the anguished Japanese public as to invite violence against Ōkuma, causing him to lose one of his legs in a bomb attack on October 18, 1889. By this time, foreign diplomats had also become greatly preoccupied with possible attacks they might suffer from the recalcitrant Japanese public. Pressures for the revision thus started to come from many directions.

The Era of Aoki

The next foreign minister, Aoki Shūzō, negotiated a treaty with the objective of regaining complete legal and tariff rights within six years. He became foreign minister in 1889, a post to be taken over by Enomoto Takeaki in 1891, and he again assumed the post in November 1898. Aoki was known as a skilled diplomat, probably the most Europeanised of all, who became engaged in the most difficult talks with the Western powers during the whole negotiation process, when the real chance for success emerged. The Anglo-Japan Treaty on Commerce and Navigation (Aoki-Kimberley Treaty) was signed right before Japan entered into war with China in 1894, when Aoki was the Japanese minister to Germany. Renouncing extraterritoriality for the first time, albeit provisionally, it proved to be the biggest achievement of his shrewd diplomacy. Of great significance in the treaty was the fact that it became the basis for extracting similar treaties from other European countries, bringing a whole group of new treaties into force within five years after the British treaty was enforced. Japan concluded similar treaties with the United States in February 1895, Germany in April 1895, Russia in June 1895, and France in August 1896. These treaties promised to abrogate extraterritoriality by 1899.

Several conditions needed to be met for these treaties to be brought into effect. For example, Japan had to completely modernise its legal systems in time to demonstrate its "standard of civilisation" to the Western powers. The civil code of 1893, which came into effect in July 1898, and the commercial code in July 1899, paved the way for those treaties to take effect and for Japan to participate in many international conferences.

Aoki's role is said to have been especially significant in obtaining consent from Germany and Belgium to end the unequal treaties. As an experienced former minister to Germany, he tried to persuade the German government that Japan qualified to have the inequality lifted. When the Germans kept pointing out the inadequacy of Japan's laws and tariff proposals, Aoki went so far as to prepare a pamphlet defending Japan's standard in meeting the requirements of a civilised legal system. He further made copies of the laws that Japan had newly introduced and delivered them to the German officials.[9] Proud of his achievement after his success in convincing the Germans, Aoki wrote to the then Foreign Minister Mutsu:

> Since I came here in February, I have had about fifty official and private conversations and have at long last clinched the talks and signed a satisfactory agreement ... In the treaty ... there may be a number of clauses that do not meet with the approval of Viscount Tani Kanjo and others but for the most part it is an understanding that is not inconvenient. Under it we can discard the insults we have suffered over the last thirty years and at once go enter the "Fellowship of Nations." Truly a matter for great congratulation. When we signed the treaty two days ago, Lord Kimberley (British Foreign Secretary) congratulated our cabinet and me, saying that "the importance of this treaty for Japan far outweighs the defeat of the great armies of China." From now on we must try to make our government and people act in accordance with "the Laws of Nations" and thereby cause civilisation to flourish increasingly in our land. ... [It] would give rise to unbounded gratification at home and abroad and would certainly reap exceptional benefits for the future. Although there are some who do not approve of the treaty, you wanted to bring it to a positive conclusion and it has conferred a myriad of gifts on our country.[10]

It was with these treaties taking effect that the long-awaited end of extraterritoriality was finally achieved in August of 1899 during the Era of Mutsu. It was the fruit of thirty years' efforts on the part of Japanese leaders.[11] At the same time, the MFN clauses in the treaties became reciprocal and unconditional. Although Japan did not acquire tariff autonomy at this time, the removal of unequal juridical treaties represented huge gains in substance and in prestige. The success in treaty negotiation in 1894 added to Japanese confidence, giving momentum to its resolution to fight against China in the Sino-Japanese War at the final stage of decisionmaking. Victory in the war further won Japan a reputation as a qualified member of international society.

The Era of Mutsu

Mutsu Munemitsu is considered a representative of Japan's *Realpolitik* of the era, and also one of the founding fathers of Japan's diplomacy, along with the previously mentioned Iwakura. He served in office from 1892 to 1896 and was also at the centre of managing the crisis at the time of the Sino-Japanese War. While he was in the United States, he served as a minister to Mexico as well, when Japan successfully signed the commercial treaty with Mexico as the first treaty signed with the West on an equal basis. Signing of the Anglo-Japanese commercial treaty in July 1894 through the mediation of Aoki was a true breakthrough in the process to lift the unequal treaties, as it had set the pattern for Japan's negotiations with the other powers who came to learn that Britain, with her large mercantile community, was ready to contemplate the ending of extraterritorial jurisdiction.

Treaty reform had become a complex political game that involved numerous domestic and foreign interests. Mutsu had to negotiate the reform while dealing with increasing domestic complaints about the unequal treaty. As the government was often criticised for its having an easygoing attitude towards foreigners, but a harsh one towards their own nationals (*gaijū naikō*), Mutsu had to be careful not to display the image that Japan was succumbing to the demands of the West.[12] Mutsu firmly believed that what Japan had been requesting in the negotiations on the treaty revision was what Japan already deserved. He also understood that complete reciprocity and mutual benefits needed to be clearly shown to the Japanese public in revising the treaty.

By this time the perceptions of treaty port merchants had started to change, too. They increasingly recognised that foreign settlements were not only inessential to expand trade in Japan any more, but also burdensome to maintain, especially since the Japanese sentiments against them had become a serious preoccupation and fear to them. Many of them, in fact, felt that "if these extraterritorial rights continued in perpetuity, it might result in a revulsion among the Japanese which would result in the loss of a large market."[10] The Japanese leaders could, therefore, effectively use the public antiforeign sentiment in persuading the West. The possibility of attack against the foreign diplomats invited significant changes in the attitudes of foreign powers during the process of treaty reform negotiations.

Mutsu also continued to negotiate secretly overseas in order to prevent the debate from leaking out to the domestic audience or to the treaty ports in Japan. In addition, he used competitions among Western powers and negotiated with the powers individually, maintaining secrecy as much as possible. Although Western powers had tended to present a united front for maintaining extraterritorial jurisdiction backed by the MFN clause, Japan by this time could divide up the jealous powers and treat the problems separately, taking advantage, for example, of the Anglo-German rivalry. The Anglo-Russian rivalry also became an advantage for Japanese leaders.

The new draft treaty approved by the cabinet in July 1893 included a procedure to bring it into effect when the legal system was fully revised, leading to the abolishment of consular jurisdiction and foreign settlements. The initial approaches were made to Germany and Britain, with Aoki in charge as the most experienced diplomat to handle the matter. In view of reluctant German attitudes, he entered into private negotiations with the British minister to Japan, Hugh Fraser (serving from 1889 to94). Meanwhile antiforeign feelings connected to the treaty revision rose so high that Britain feared that the Japanese government might be forced to take strong measures over the revision problem. On the part of Japan, the approaching crisis of the Sino-Japanese war encouraged the leaders to hasten to conclude the treaty. The treaty was finally signed on July 16, 1894. It consisted of three documents, including the lifting of extraterritoriality five years after the signing.

The Sino-Japanese War and Japan's Appeal to the West

As negotiations with the West were becoming increasingly complicated games of balancing external and domestic pressures, East Asian international politics were in the process of immense structural change. The Sino-Japanese War became a great opportunity for Japan to impress the West with its level of civilisation, especially in observing the multilateral treaties it had negotiated. Japan had become the first Asian country to join in the Treaty of Geneva (Treaty of the Red Cross) in 1886.[14] The Treaty of Geneva included articles on the rules of humanitarian activities for wounded soldiers beyond national borders, prohibiting attack on them even during wartime. According to Takahashi Sakue, the signing of these treaties assured the Western powers of Japan's degree of civilisation. The Western powers, however, were not sure about Japan's capability to observe the treaties at the time of war. It was through the Sino-Japanese War and the Russo-Japanese War that Japan's compliance with international law won their assurance and trust.

China and Japan declared war on August 1, 1894, fighting over the requests that Korea made to China to help them suppress the rebels. Japan emphasised its altruistic motive to protect Korea's independence and need for modernisation from its backward suzerain, China.[15] In insisting on Korean independence, Japan stuck to the Tienjing Treaty of 1885, in which Itō had negotiated the terms of withdrawal from the

Korean peninsula with China, referring to international law as guidance.[16] It was an experiment of the Japanese "standard of civilisation" to be evaluated by the West, since the war proceeded in parallel with the treaty revision as a test for Japan's physical and civilian power that would make it qualify as a member of international society.

Up until the Sino-Japanese War, most of the Japanese studies on international law were focused on the import of Western concepts and practices through precise translation and meticulous study of them. Original Japanese writing on international law, especially on laws of war, started to appear, however, around the time of the Sino-Japanese War. Ariga Nagao's *Bankoku Senji Kōhō* (International Laws of War) in 1894 and Nakamura Shingo's *Kōwa Ruirei* (Cases of Peace Treaties) in 1895 are such examples.[17] The establishment of the Japanese Association for International Law and Diplomacy in 1897, ten years earlier than its US equivalent, the American Association for International Law, also indicates Japan's keen interest in further development of the study of international law. At the time of its establishment, the association mostly concentrated on the study of the laws of war.

In their victorious war against China, Japanese soldiers were instructed to observe international law faithfully and to avoid any conduct that might invite accusations of violating these codes. They had spent a great amount of time learning international law at military college. Before the war, Aoki "tried to educate British public opinion by using *The Times,* the *Daily Telegraph,* and the *Daily Chronicle* to gain acceptance for Japan's activities."[18] Japan also made great efforts to record and make known its faithful adherence to international law in waging the war. At the initial stage of the Sino-Japanese War, Prime Minister Ito ordered several international lawyers including Ariga Nagao, Takahashi Sakue, and Shinoda Harusaku, to accompany the military and write about the lawfulness of Japan's declaration of war and the conduct of its imperial army. In order to convince the European powers that the war was carried out lawfully by Japan, they needed to use the language of international law properly. Ariga in his *La guerre sino-japonaise au point de vue du droit international* (The Sino-Japanese War in Light of International Law) faithfully described the laws of war related to the ongoing conflict between China and Japan and argued that Japan participated in the war lawfully, emphasising the army's observance of all the major articles of international law.[19]

Not only did Ariga appeal to the West by displaying the lawfulness of the conduct of the Japanese army, but he also contrasted Japan's behaviour with that of China as "unlawful" behaviour. Ariga mentioned that a critical feature of the war between China and Japan was that one party (Japan) strictly followed international law, while another (China) never observed any legal practice of war. Moreover, Ariga stated that Japan's unilateral observance in a case where mutual observance of international law was impossible showed the obligation to humankind that Japan was demonstrating.[20] He insistently emphasised that Japan never sacrificed its faithful observance of law in pursuing its strategic gains and that the war between Japan and China set a precedent for wars between the "civilised" and the "uncivilised."[21]

Similarly, Takahashi Sakuye appealed to the international community by arguing that Japan always adhered to international law in waging the war and in protecting its interests. Relying on international legal terms and logic, he also stated that the spirit of obeying the law had been a traditional characteristic of the Japanese. In his *Cases on International Law During the Chino-Japanese War*, prefaced by T. E. Holland and introduced by John Westlake, both representing the authority of positive international law, he wrote a section on "the law-abiding spirit of Japan in carrying on hostilities" in the introductory chapter. He stated that the spirit was embedded in Japan since older times.

> It must be confessed that this generosity is chiefly owed to European civilisation, which was introduced thirty years ago, but in general it may be said that if the graft was from Europe, the stock was an ancient one, deep-rooted in Japan from the earliest times. [22]

Like Ariga, Takahashi also took the view that the Sino-Japanese War was a war between "civilised" Japan and "uncivilised" China.[23] He criticised China's not joining the Treaty of Geneva or the Paris Declaration and its "barbarian" conduct of the war. He was on solid ground in stating this, as the Japanese Red Cross had helped one hundred thousand injured and sick people during the Sino-Japanese War, including many Chinese, while being constantly attacked by China. Their dedication and efficiency was highly praised by the European powers, contributing greatly to the reputation of Japan as a legitimate "civilised" country qualified to join the European club of international society.[24]

T.E. Holland mentions Japan's faithful observance of international law during the Sino-Japanese War, contrasting Japan to China.[25] Similarly,

Westlake states that Japan shed its semicivilised status by developing the same legal systems as civilised European nations.

> Japan presents a rare and interesting example of the passage of a state from the oriental to the European class. By virtue of treaties already concluded with the leading Christian states of Europe and America, she will shortly be freed from the institution of consular jurisdiction, and in her recent war with China she displayed both the disposition and in the main the ability to observe Western rules concerning war and neutrality.[26]

Further, Wheaton in his fourth edition of *Elements of International Law* (1904) stated that Japan achieved a complete membership and status in international society. In the section entitled "International status of non-Christian countries," he mentioned that Japan participated in important international conventions, including the 1866 Geneva Convention and the 1899 Hague Conference, that Japan fought a war against China according to "the highest standard of civilisation," that Japan revised domestic civil and criminal codes "so that as of 1899 all persons of whatever nationality within the confines of Japan have been subject to the Japanese tribunals," that it abrogated extraterritoriality by 1899, and that it became a British ally in 1902.[27] Other international lawyers such as Oppenheim and Phillimore recognised Japan's observance of international law and practices, too.[28]

It was due to these efforts that had extended over the years, however, that the Triple Intervention by Russia, Germany, and France in 1895 turned out to be even more humiliating an experience than it might have been otherwise. When they demanded that Japan return the Liaodong Peninsula, Tokutomi Sohō said, "What it came down to was that sincerity or justice didn't amount to a thing if you weren't strong enough ... After conforming wholeheartedly to the spirit and letter of international law and diplomacy, Japan seemed forced to conclude that, in the end, only force mattered in international relations."[29] The ending of the Sino-Japanese War, therefore, eventually became a threshold to Japan's joining of the European colonial competition. The bitterness and the humiliation was felt all the more because of the efforts that Japan had made in complying with the Western standard of civilisation, sometimes even sacrificing national pride.[30] Japan's encounter with the West and the conformity with international law during the negotiation process for the treaty revision, thus, in a way sowed the seeds of Japanese diplomacy that led up to the early Showa.

Conclusion: Abrogation of Unequal Treaties

At the end of the nineteenth century, Japan engaged in the most enthusiastic diplomatic activities in its history. The ending of the unequal treaties was a slower process than had been expected. One reason for this was the concern of the treaty powers, which naturally wanted to maintain the extraterritoriality privileges as long as possible to protect the lives and rights of their citizens. Even up to the late 1880s, therefore, many Westerners still felt that extraterritoriality was necessary.[31] While the treaties could have been officially revised as early as 1872 during the Iwakura Mission, it took many more years of negotiation before the final abrogation. Japan's fast Westernisation and rise to the status of great power often obscures the struggles that the nation went through. Examination of the process of Japan's socialisation into international society reveals that it was no miracle but rather a consequence of a realistic combination of what was available for Japan and what the leaders tried to achieve.

The pressures that Japan placed on itself in modernising its domestic systems, especially after the Iwakura Mission, propelled Japan's development, which was helped even further by the strong determination of the political leaders. Statesmen like Inoue, Ōkuma, Aoki, and Mutsu found it politically necessary to create various institutions, such as civil and criminal codes, and a system of justice according to the European model. Ōkuma made a speech at the Diet while he was a foreign minister in December of 1897:

> Having devoted herself for years with ardour and diligence to national progress, and having come to enjoy the great friendship of the Powers of Europe and America, Japan, which for forty years past has been fettered with disadvantageous treaties, has now advanced to such a position that she, in conformity with international usage, is accorded the treatment of an equal. This is, in fact, the result of her own progress, and of England's consent, leading the rest of the world, to a revision of the existing treaties.[32]

As we have seen, Japan had grasped the gist of positivist international law with relative accuracy from the early period of its adoption. The positivism that Japan had learned since the 1860s was applied to its foreign policy during the 1890s. Obvious in the writings of Japanese international lawyers of this period is the constant drawing on the actual written laws as well as the application of those laws in actual practice. Japan's national behaviour as a civilised state was thus displayed in a most convincing way to the eyes of the West, including Takahashi Sakue's adoption of the "Harvard method" of case studies in his writings.[33]

Japan found ways to use the international norm of the period, the standard of civilisation, to convince the domestic audience. While the rise of nationalism certainly made it difficult for the leaders to control the negotiation process, it had positive effects, too. The leaders could use the pressures from domestic patriotism and emphasise the necessity of giving in to foreign demands in order to maintain Japanese independence. The Japanese leaders, in turn, used nationalism to convince the international community as an excuse for the need for early abrogation of extraterritoriality. Antiforeign sentiments, in fact, were becoming a threat to foreigners living in Japan. Treaty port merchants were especially afraid of losing their big market because of the hatred against foreign goods. Here the cost-benefit calculation of the great powers started to change, working favourably towards early abrogation.

In parallel with the treaty revision negotiations, Aoki repeatedly "called the attention of the British government to Korean affairs and tried to prevent it from leaning towards China."[34] He skillfully persuaded the Western powers of Japan's rights to occupy Korea by using the international logic and terms that would most appeal to them. He drew frequently on the Tienjing Treaty of 1885. Numerous letters and memoranda exchanged among Japanese officials reveal their mastery of the Western sense of conducting international affairs. Their proficiency in English is also impressive, often sounding as if they had been part of the European international system for centuries.[35] Afraid that the spirit of the Tienjing Treaty might be violated, Mutsu even talked about "balance of power" between Japan and China as something to be maintained.

While the leaders negotiated the abrogation of extraterritoriality, they had to cope with and balance numerous factors that came into play: the increasing importance of public opinion concomitant with the establishment of the Diet, great power rivalry, power balance in East Asia, and incidents involving international law that highlighted the salience of the issue. The multifaceted nature of Japan's foreign policy during this period required the leaders to employ realism in muddling through the hurdles to win international status. They had two major agenda items to be cleared in order to convince the West of Japan's qualification for full membership in international society. First, they needed to actually meet the standard. Second, they needed to persuade the West that it met the standard. The leaders made sure that no violation of international law occurred in its conduct of foreign policy and that they actually sought to support the Western norm as in the case of the Red Cross and Japan's treatment of war prisoners. The leaders of early Meiji skillfully and effectively appealed for the recognition of what they had achieved.

After the pressing national goal to lift extraterritoriality was achieved in 1899, Japan continued to exhibit its pious compliance with international law at least up to the Russo-Japanese War. The materials from the National Archive of The Hague record Japan's solid observance of international law and respect for the international community. At the 1899 Hague conference, the agenda of which included pacific settlement of international disputes and laws and customs of land and naval warfare, Japan was one of the few Asian countries that participated and voiced its opinions. According to the table that shows the ratification dates of participating countries, Japan ratified all the conventions on October 6, 1900, about the same time as the European states did. As of January 1904, China and Turkey had signed but not ratified the conventions.[36] While Asian participants tend to be relatively quiet during the sessions, the record shows that the Japanese delegation occasionally voiced its views based on international law, for example, on the wording of the draft of the convention on the use of arms.[37] Anand notes that, of the five Asian countries attending, "only Japan had an effective voice in international affairs."[38]

Further, Japan developed its good reputation as a devout observer of international rules and morality by conducting no plundering or looting at the time of the Boxer Rebellion, when such acts were typical of other armies. At the time of the rebellions, Austria, Britain, France, Germany, Italy, Japan, Russia, and the United States sent troops, each in charge of a different area after they occupied Beijing. While they were supposed to be troops of "justice," countries other than Japan robbed and killed on an unprecedented scale. No rapes or robberies occurred in Japan's area, enabling the Chinese to return to the area and recover from the disaster much earlier than elsewhere.[39] The Boxer Rebellion also imprinted the West with Japan's ability to contain domestic turmoil, contrasting it with China. Gong notes that "the Boxer outrage against the comity of nations was… of sufficient gravity to make uncertain China's ability to uphold the standard of 'civilisation.'" "In the eye of the West, the contrast [between Japan and China] was clear."[40]

The Japanese leaders' earnest adherence to international law seems strikingly different from some of their counterparts thirty years later, who relied on spiritualism and blind loyalism in directing Japan's national course. If conformity to international society constitutes the main theme of "Act I" of Japan's modern diplomatic history, the theme of "Act II" would be Japan's asocial behaviour; that is, the rise of imperialism and its break with the League of Nations in later years. The Meiji leaders' realism was predicated on their nonideological assessment of Japan's status in the power configuration of international politics and their readiness to act on expediency. For the sake of the national objective, they flexibly modified the political and social systems according to what was required by the European "standard of civilisation." As Japan joined the last phase of imperialist competition in the 1930s, when imperialism was actually becoming outmoded, the leaders misperceived the gradual changes of international norms, failing to correctly assess the national capability of Japan in relation to the other great powers. The organisational structure of the leadership and factional strife in the army further blinded them in directing the country based on the balance between international and domestic constraints. While Japan's previous conformity to international norms resulted from the congruity between the systemic imperatives and domestic attributes contrived by effective leadership, its later dissociation from international society resulted from the failure to construct such congruity between them.

PART THREE

The Logic of Conformity

6 Japan's Entry in Perspective

This chapter extracts several essential features of Japan's socialisation into international society from the previous historical studies and frames Japan's socialisation process in the larger institutional dynamics of the international system. Japan's entry brought unintended consequences to Japan itself as well as to the international system. After discussing some factors to explain the nation's compliance with international norms in the first part of the chapter, I will speculate in the latter part on the relations between Japan's socialisation as a newcomer and the changes that it brought to the international system.

Conformity Variables

State socialisation and conformity to international norms is the product of domestic and international factors combined. Domestically, Japan possessed capacity and will that enabled its socialisation. Externally, those domestic attributes were tested by and fitted into the overarching international norm of the period that led the country to conformity. I will highlight here the internal and external logic of state socialisation implied in Japan's case that could be applied to other cases. The studies on Japan's conformance with the norms of international law and the "standard of civilisation" in the previous chapters have revealed several features that had not been adequately marked in the conventional view on its engagement with European international society.

Existence of Functional Equivalents

During the late nineteenth century, entry into international society was closely tied to the degree of domestic development and of meeting the standard of "civilised" Europe. The question of entry, therefore, lay at the intersection of international politics and state building, in contrast to the previous historical era, when a state's internal logic defined statehood, and the later era, when the international systemic logic started to weigh more on the nature of statehood. One who is used to the idea of a "European vs. non-European" categorisation might feel uncomfortable in locating an entity that does not fit into this divide. Japan possessed domestic institutions that could be easily translated into Western equivalents and was physically prepared to meet the Western challenge. Historians had recognised this for quite a while[1] and nowadays take it as common knowledge that the level of economic and social development in Japan at the time of its first encounters with the West far surpassed that in other non-Western countries. Japan's "modernisation" was a slow process, which had started centuries before the West's arrival, while its Westernisation was a rapid one.

The existence of domestic institutions functionally consistent with accepted practices of international society entail lower transaction costs than those that conflict with them. A country's degree of centralisation, educational level, and sources and nature of authority (military or civil, single or dual) before modern state building, for example, affect the way a country adopts Western state-apparatuses such as a military bureaucracy, a tax system, nationalism, and an educational system. In the case of Japan, cultural and religious homogeneity, a high level of education, skilled workers, a wide network of economic exchanges, and accurate knowledge of the outside world had already characterised the society by the time the West arrived. Tokyo, which was then called Edo, had become the largest city in the world by the late seventeenth century. Japanese literacy rates in the first half of the nineteenth century also compared favourably with those of Western countries.[2]

The autobiography of Fukuzawa Yukichi, an educator during early Meiji and a strong advocate of enlightenment and Westernisation, contains numerous vivid descriptions of the excitement that Japanese leaders felt during the Iwakura Mission. He mentions, however, how bored the Japanese delegation felt when the factory manager in San Francisco tried to explain the mechanisms of some factory equipment and the principles of plating or boiling water during their stay in the United States, the first Western country that they had ever seen. "We all knew about them, but they were so proud to be teaching us something they thought we didn't know," he writes.[3] Fukuzawa records that the Japanese delegation was more impressed with the social customs, life-style, wealth, social principles, and concepts of "rights" and "democracy" in the United States than the level of Western science and technology.[4] The level of technological advancement in Japan can also be surmised by the fact that they made their own ships only a couple of years after they first saw the American fleet in 1853. Fukuzawa, in fact, visited the United States on board the first Japanese ship that crossed the Pacific, the *Kanrinmaru*, before he accompanied the Iwakura Mission.

Economically, while the domain system was based on heavily overtaxed agricultural production, other undertaxed sectors were allowed to grow more freely.

> The wholesale merchants and entrepreneurs of the big cities prospered enormously in the seventeenth century. ... By the nineteenth century the Japanese probably had the most advanced and thoroughly monetized economy in Asia and were well prepared for further economic development. They had, therefore, little trouble understanding and adopting the commercial and industrial patterns of the West – and there again they had a running start at modernization.[5]

As we have seen in Chapter 1, the validity of applying traditional concepts such as "modern" and "feudal" to the Japanese context is often called into question by revisionist historians. Considering Meiji as a watershed between feudalism and modernity in Japanese history has increasingly become a minority view. M. Bito, for example, views the sixteenth century as the key historical juncture at which the modern territorial entity of Japan emerged.[6] Economic historians, in particular, emphasise the continuity between the pre- and post-Meiji Restoration periods and argue that contemporary market-oriented society in Japan has its origins in the Tokugawa era or even earlier.[7]

The existence of the imperial institution since the ancient times in Japan has also played a significant role in facilitating modernisation. According to Sven Steinmo and Kathleen Thelen, one of the situations where institutional dynamism is observed is when "previously latent institutions suddenly become salient, with implications for political outcomes."[8] The Japanese imperial institution, which had been obscured for centuries, served as such a latent institution that suddenly became available and was highlighted as an alternative political authority with the crisis brought about with the arrival of the West and with the subsequent overthrow of the domain system under the Tokugawa political regime. Japan could justify and use the imperial institution by restoring it and dignifying it to a symbolic venerability as a native institution easily accepted by the public. Proimperial sentiment, which had existed long before Perry came, was reactivated as the Westernisation process started.

The domestic institutions conducive to national development were not limited to tangible ones. Intangible resources that might be called "social capital" also expedited the modernisation process. A sense of responsibility for society and the state that was widely shared in Japan is often said to originate in the military (*samurai*) ethic of devoting oneself to the public good, thus enabling the country to act together effectively for the national purpose.[9] Coordinated actions were facilitated by the existence of trustworthiness and social networks accompanied by a sense of obligation to the country. A relatively advanced printing culture had also contributed to creation of a "public sphere."[10] The social capital arguments that explain economic performance, the level of democracy, or effective government can thus be applied to explaining Japan's socialisation, its nation building, and its foreign policy behaviour. It is argued that countries with social capital in general demonstrate a greater sense of obligation and cooperation for the provision of international public goods, more sensitivity to expectations by other countries, and more loyal compliance with international norms.[11]

Further, congruity in mechanism between international and domestic institutions enables the country to make the existing domestic institutions, whether physical, human, or social, conform to the international necessity. The domestic institutions culturally different from the West, but equivalent in institutional mechanism, can be called "functional equivalents," which could be recreated, reorganised, and modified so they would fit into the Western mould. Noting the importance of domestic infrastructures that had already existed in Japan before the West's arrival, Kohno Masaru argues that Japan was already "sovereign" when the West arrived.[12] Drawing on the Namamugi Incident of 1862,[13] he emphasises the fact that Japan was already capable of crossborder movements and of exercising public authority, and that Western countries treated Japan as sovereign. He sheds light on Japan's debated international status during the nineteenth century, which had been overlooked in the stereotypical divide between the civilised vs. the uncivilised, and European vs. non-European.

The abundant existence of "functional equivalents," however, does not alone constitute a sufficient condition for the ultimate objective of obtaining full membership in international society. Since sovereignty is a relational concept, it needs to be expressed externally and achieved through recognition by other members of international society. The biggest challenge for Japan as a prospective member of the society was this external dimension of sovereignty. Through treaty negotiations and appeals to the West, Japan became vigourously engaged in the external dimension of sovereignty.

Expediency and Manipulations

Another feature of Japan's socialisation is that Japanese leaders acted more on the basis of national self-interests than had conventionally been believed in manipulating and manoeuvring the course of their country's affairs in achieving international status. While loyally respecting international law, their attitudes evolved over time. In contrast to their infatuation with the West in the early period of modernisation, they eventually started to hold sceptical views of international law and learned that it was, in fact, Janus-faced: it could be a shield for the weak, facilitating reciprocity and protecting equality among nations, but it could also be an instrument of the strong to dominate the weak. Japan's conformity to Western norms, therefore, gradually became more hardboiled and instrumental. The way a country socialises and complies with international law is quite often so nuanced that it does not always afford a dichotomy between "acceptance and rejection."[14] It should rather be explained on a continuum of different degrees of conformance. Nish's portrait of Iwakura manifests the essence of such complex aspects of socialisation.

> Responsive to new ideas from the outside world, he was still determined to control any foreign ideas adopted. Although he admired foreign countries, he was basically scared of them and their ambitions towards Japan. Conservative and nationalist, he was at the same time flexible and a modernizer. His contribution to Japan's foreign relations lay not so much in policies as in attitudes: he led Japan to the 'realistic' policy of cautious and vigilant, even hesitant, acceptance of the West.[15]

At the early stage of encounters with the West, there was a practical need for Japan to convince the public of the necessity to increase national power by unifying the country, especially in order to cope with the domestic turmoil that the country had been experiencing since the eighteenth century.[16] The need to open up the nation could be used as a way of solving domestic problems. Lifting of unequal treaties was also an economic must for Japan, which needed to expand trade and enrich the nation, on top of a symbolic necessity to be recognised as one of the great powers in the European club. Antiforeign attitudes during the early period needed to be transformed into energy for creating a new modern nation by revising unequal treaties and obtaining the deserved international status. For that purpose, Japan actually used the foreign threat by exaggerating it. The foreign threat became "a valuable neurosis for a new nation-state, which kept the need for national defence very much before the people and urged on them the necessary sacrifices.[17]" When it became clear that national independence was no longer in jeopardy, Japan's course was clearly set: open up the country, end the *bakufu*, unite the country under an emperor, modernise by vigourously adopting Western technology, engage in domestic political reforms, and eventually join the Western powers in colonial conquests. Since not all of the nation's energy needed to be consumed for survival, leaders could engage in national development and in achieving international status in the European club of great powers.

We have seen that, in negotiating treaties with Korea and China, the Japanese leaders consciously used English and referred to the "law of nations" as a guiding rule of negotiations.[18] Demonstrating its compliance with international law, including the technicalities of language use, they were also able to modify and reorganise power relations in East Asia, which had traditionally centred around China. The positivism as the gist of international law that Japan had grasped since the 1860s was applied for rationalising its foreign policy during the period starting in the 1870s.

Iriye Akira emphasises the traditional Sinic notions of world order embedded in the minds of Japanese leaders and the importance of Chinese learning as a prerequisite for them. Referring to the backwardness of the thinking of the Japanese leaders, he claims that they in fact relied on Chinese translations of the treaties.[19] The documentation of Japanese foreign affairs at the Foreign Record Office and the materials on the international conferences that Japan has participated in since the late nineteenth century in The Hague show, however, the exceptional talents of the Meiji political leaders versed in Western languages and in legal knowledge that are at least comparable to those of the most capable foreign officers today.[20]

The leaders increasingly had to deal with rising nationalism and public sentiment against the unequal treaties from around 1880. Particularly with the promulgation of the Constitution, the treaty revision problem became a precarious game where complex domestic and international factors intertwined. As we have seen in Chapter 5, the leaders used domestic politics to pressure the West, while employing foreign pressure to convince the domestic audience of the need to pursue modern nation building. In order to avoid being swayed by domestic opinions, they negotiated in foreign capitals. They also exploited the competition among the Western powers, negotiating with each country separately.

In the 1890s, several government-appointed Japanese scholars produced works that rationalised Japan's conduct of foreign relations from the perspectives of international law. Obvious in the work of those international lawyers, such as Ariga and Takahashi, was the constant reliance on and reference to the actual written laws in recording Japanese foreign policy practice. They displayed Japan's behaviour as that of a civilised state in a most convincing and appealing way in the eyes of the West. The manipulations of Japanese leaders in dealing with domestic politics as well as foreign relations were based on their accurate understanding of the prevalent international norms that they had to conform to and the clear sense of direction in which they wanted to lead their country.

It had been a common understanding that, when the gap between the European and non-European standards needed to be bridged, it was bridged by the imposition of the former on the "uncivilised" latter. As this study as well as many other recent works on colonialism and European expansionism have revealed, however, a monolithic view of European imposition of their norms is unwarranted. The European standards were in fact digested, recreated, adapted, and transformed into something that newcomer states could eventually use as a tool to enhance their national interests. More active learning and more choices were present on the part of non-Western countries in meeting with the Western "standard," taking on different styles; calculation, self-interest, and rationalisation accompanied the compliance processes. As Japan's case indicates, latecomers more often than not use the existing international norm to direct their transition from novices to fully sovereign states and do not remain recipients of prevalent norms. Norm dynamics literature also often notes that local agents frequently promote norm diffusion and do not remain passive targets of it. They not only reconstruct the prevalent norms, but also try to build congruence between the norm and their domestic logic.[21]

Congruence-building between domestic and international logic becomes a major task of political leaders and the key to socialisation. The roles of leaders are important especially because "new norms never enter a normative vacuum but instead emerge in a highly contested normative space where they must compete with other norms and perceptions of interest."[22] Japanese political leaders had to cope with such "normative contestation" by calculating the cost of inappropriate action and by balancing it against the benefit of compliance.[23] The roles of the leaders were salient in reconciling and coordinating the competing norms to create logical consistency between the international and the domestic.

Systemic Constraints of the Nineteenth-Century International System

One last, most dominant feature of Japan's socialisation is the positivist international norm that characterised the particular historical period. While the conventional wisdom has identified Japan as a prize pupil of modernisation and Westernisation, taking an agentic view and emphasising the peculiarity and uniqueness of the country, it was the international environment of nineteenth-century international society that played an overarching role in defining the course of Japan. As the prevailing studies on modernisation and nation building tend to focus on the socialisees, few studies have analysed the constraints that newcomers receive from the norms of international society in the particular historical stage of institutionalisation of the sovereign state system.

The modern European state system that emerged as a Westphalian system in the seventeenth century was consolidated during the nineteenth century with the development of the Eurocentric "standard of civilisation" and positivist international law. The socioeconomic change that occurred as exogenous environmental change defined the power configuration of the world, empowering Europe with respect to other parts of the world. In outlining several characteristics of the European expansion, Jörg Fisch notes that in no time in history did "legal and moral justification [play] such an important part. The Europeans tried hard to legitimise their actions, to find a solid legal foundation for what they did rather than simply to refer to a right of conquest."[24]

As briefly discussed in Chapter 2, the ascendancy of positive international law discarded "some of the fundamental qualities of the classic Law of Nations, particularly the principle of the universality of the Family of Nations based on Christianity irrespective of creed, colour, and continent," thus rendering international law "shrinking" from a universal order into an Eurocentric one.[25] The legal practice of the European states became the basis of law.

By the positivist turn, international law reidentified itself for further adaptation to the new international environment, posing unique norms of statehood on the newcomer states, among which was the "standard of civilisation." Positivist writers such as Henry Wheaton, William E. Hall, James Lorimer, Thomas Lawrence, M. F. Lindley, T. E. Holland, John Westlake, and Lassa Oppenheim articulated the positive international law and "standard of civilisation" in response to the questions that arose in the course of European contact with increasing numbers of non-European countries.[26]

> Positivism was the new analytic apparatus used by the jurists of the time to account for the events that culminated in the universalisation of international law and the formulation of a body of principles that was understood to apply globally as a result of the annexation of unoccupied territories such as the Australian continent, the conquest of large parts of Asia, and the partitioning of Africa.[27]

Legal positivism was based on the distinction between civilised and noncivilised states. It was based on a teleological interpretation of the world that every country is to become civilised eventually and that a country obtains rights in accordance with its degree of civilisation.[28] As international law was to be applied only to the sovereign states civilised in the European sense, the empowered European states needed to determine the conditions for admitting non-European political entities to the membership of the international community that they themselves formed. The increase of national power became synonymous with European civilisation as well as the indicator of meeting the European standard; conformity to European norms and conventions became objectives of non-European countries that tried to enter the European club of nations. As the West demanded that Japan demonstrate national power as a legitimate member of the international society of great powers, the military in particular became a significant expression of the capacity and the will of the nation. This explains Japan's rapid armament as well as its concentration on the learning of the laws of war in adopting Western international law, and its eventual participation in the colonial competition with other Western powers. As Tilly's famous thesis suggests, Japan as a latecomer faced more systemic constraints than the early members of the West in international society.[29] Japanese leaders needed to learn the historically contingent Euro-dominant norm of the nineteenth century and accept the positivist norm of international law, which all the other non-European countries came to conform to during this era.[30]

Studies on Japanese history have often blinded us to systemic forces that operate at the global level. To see the whole picture of the Japanese process of socialisation and entry into international society, we need to frame history in a structure that embodies the power distribution and the nature of international relations of the nineteenth century and to consider the systemic imperative entailed. It was under this positivist pressure that Japan braced itself against a possible invasion by the West and vectored its existing "functional equivalents" towards the Western sense of modernisation and compliance with international law. This study has, thus, emphasised context and structure over agents, while also taking into account the agentic variables in explaining how a newcomer responded to the normative constraints of the international system. Domestic variables such as the level of development in social infrastructures and perceptions of leaders operate as intervening variables between the international structure and the outcome of the foreign policy.

In studies of institutions, scholars' emphases vary from the crude rational-choice variant that focuses on choices of the human agent on the one end of the continuum to the historical institutionalist variant that focuses more on the constraints imposed on actors within specific historical contexts on the other end.[31] With regard to interpretations of the behavioural logic of actors, the former is characterised by individualism and instrumentalism and the latter by notions of obligations and responsibilities. While the utility-maximising logic that underlies the rational choice approaches had been contrasted against what social constructivists call "the logic of appropriateness, in which actors internalise roles and rules as scripts to which they conform,"[32] the rational choices by the actors and the norms that constrain them are, in fact, inextricably related. As individual choices are always made in a given social environment, the behavioural logic itself cannot be discussed in any meaningful way nor explained fully without mentioning the social structure where the agent is placed. Shared norms, expectations, and beliefs about "appropriate behaviour" can be the basis for acting rationally and for promoting national interest. Actors may make rational choice among contesting norms or "appropriate behaviours," or aim at constructing new appropriate norms by rational choice.[33] Acknowledging the importance of clarification of causal directions in enhancing explanatory power of the theory and the possibility of leaving readers with the impression of indeterminacy there, I find it necessary, therefore, to investigate contextual and agentic variables eclectically in order to unravel a country's logic of conformity.

Socialisation and Institutionalisation Dynamics

The Meaning of Entry into International Society for Japan

Japan's socialisation with international society brought with it several consequences, both positive and negative, for the future course of the nation. Under nineteenth-century international law, Japan received an incentive for modern nation building, as the prevalent norm then necessitated that nation building and entry into international society be a simultaneous processes. With all the unjust, unequal treatment, and insults that Japan had endured during the negotiation process of the unequal treaties, and with all the frustrations and resentment it bore in order to be admitted to the European club, it was endowed with opportunities for creating modern statehood. At no time in history were the incentives for crafting sovereign statehood stronger than during the late nineteenth century. It was only under the strong pressure from the Eurocentric "standard of civilisation" that Japanese "functional equivalents" could be remoulded and recreated so they would fit the Western mould.

One striking feature of the process of the nineteenth-century adaptation of the sovereign state system is that African and Asian countries as newcomers all embraced the Euro-dominant rules of international society, even though they often contradicted their style. During the period of European expansion and colonisation of the globe, Asian and African leaders complied to various degrees with the norms of international society, including political organisations, international law, diplomatic customs and procedures, military technology, the concept of sovereignty, and democracy.

Becoming a member of the European club during the nineteenth century itself meant becoming a modern, "civilised" state. International recognition meant having achieved a certain level of national development that accorded with that of the West. Compared with the long, violent process of state building in Europe, or with that of today's third-world countries, which can easily enter international society but tend to face enormous difficulties in achieving effective internal governance in the absence of external incentives, Japan's entry and national development was achieved relatively efficiently and peacefully.[34] It was the systemic imperative of the positivist norm that facilitated Japan's national development and achievement of international status.

Nation building is thus an historically contingent endeavour. The international norms of different historical periods define the *problematique* of statehood and state building. How to respond to the historical contingency depends, as we have seen, on the attributes of a country, including its physical preparedness as well as its leaders' capacity to build congruence between domestic logic and the systemic imperative of international society.

Today's nation building encounters a problem quite different from that of the nineteenth century; states that do not have *de facto* control and jurisdiction or states that lack capacity to meet even such a basic international norm as human rights are allowed to survive. In other words, no single "standard" exists for countries to conform to in obtaining membership in international society. Heterogeneity in the level of civilisation, development, and national strength is preserved on entering international society. Consequently, the death rates of states today have dramatically declined with the prevalent norm of the right to self-determination, nonaggression, and *de jure* equality of sovereignty. Statehood requires only defined territory and international recognition today.[35]

This change in the nature of statehood brought serious consequences to nation building in less developed countries. Prospective newcomers to international society today do not enjoy as many motivations for effective national governance as did those in previous periods. While effective nation building and socialisation with international society were simultaneous processes during the nineteenth century, nation building has become irrelevant to obtaining membership in the contemporary international society.[36]

Nation building and modernisation was something that involved alterations in all aspects of the Japanese lifestyle. When the Iwakura Mission was sent to the United States, the president told the Japanese delegation that Western custom dictated Western dress and hairstyles. Accordingly, Iwakura himself had his topknot (*chonmage*) cut off during the mission after a US newspaper criticised his "adherence to the Japanese style."[37] From today's standpoint, it is difficult to imagine how the delegation could tolerate such a decree without taking it as humiliation and as something that goes against cultural relativism and mutual respect. This type of dictate was possible only under the dominant nineteenth-century positivism.

One critically important feature of Japan's entry, however, was that Japan achieved modern statehood without changing its cultural fabric. Behavioural compliance rather than internalisation is what characterised Japan's entry into international society, which perhaps applies to the entry of other newcomer states as well. The previously mentioned change in hairstyle and lifestyle rather belongs to behavioural compliance, which is instrumental and practical. While critics have often called it a superficial adoption of Western norms, few countries in fact ever truly internalise the norms of others in the course of compliance. Although various degrees and levels of adoption and adaptation occur during the process of state socialisation, it is doubtful whether internalisation is necessary for compliance with international norms. In his critique of Kai Alderson's theory of state socialisation, Cameron G. Thies makes this point clear:

> [No] matter how hard members try, novices do not internalize norms, rather they simply alter their behaviour to avoid sanctions ... It will often be the case that states do not alter their identities, interests, or behaviour as a result of internalizing the norms promulgated by other member states in the international system. Sometimes they alter their behaviour for strategic reasons, or they may simply adapt in order to avoid negative consequences ... Placing socialization and rational action at opposite ends of a continuum is not theoretically justified, nor is it necessarily empirically accurate.[38]

The flood of Western knowledge was equally met by the same level of cultural coherence during the era of social upheavals of epic proportions in Japan. Retention of cultural integrity was in fact another side of the coin of Japan's vigourous efforts to adopt Western civilisation. It was critically important for the unity of the country to find ways to conform to international norms without jeopardising its cultural independence.

Socialisation of Japan and Institutionalisation of the Sovereign State System

While it is difficult to be precise about the effects of Japan's socialisation on international society, one can speculate about some impacts that it brought to the community of states. First, Japan's socialisation reaffirmed the European dominance of international society, contributing to further "autonomy" and "coherence" of the international system as an institution, whose "adaptability" was to continue to be tested by new environmental challenges. One of the consequences of the positivist turn of international law was the emergence of the Eurocentric concept of a "standard of civilisation," a development that enhanced the integrity and legitimacy of the European state system. While the expansion of the originally European international society may have looked like an open process, where newcomer states gradually became accepted as members, it also led to reinforcement of the European standards that newcomer states came to comply with. European dominance was not only maintained, but also in a way enhanced by the entrance of newcomers. Anghie mentions that the recognition of non-European states as sovereign

> was not merely, or even primarily, concerned with ascertaining or establishing the legal status of the entity under scrutiny; rather it was about affirming the power of the European states to claim sovereignty, to reinforce their authority to make such determinations, and consequently, to make sovereignty a possession that they could then proceed to dispense, deny, create, or grant partially ... Recognition does not so much resolve the problem of determining the status of unknown entities as obscure the history of the process by which this decision-making framework came into being.[39]

Similarly, Gong describes Japan's conforming behaviour as a turning point where the European standard was reaffirmed.

> When Japan gained recognition as a civilized power by adhering to it, the standard of civilization took its place as a universally valid principle, applicable to all non-European countries seeking to enter the Family of Nations as civilized states.[40]

Second, not only did Japan's entry increase the "autonomy" of the international system as an institution, it also helped international society incorporate "complexity" and "durability" as institutions, facilitating the socialisation of other non-European states. For the European sovereign state-system, the entry of Japan, a non-European power that shared hardly any common culture, came as an exogenous shock. Japan's entry occurred as the European-dominant *Gemeinschaft* gradually began to transform itself into a global *Geselleschaft* consisting of diverse members that shared only the legal minimum of sovereignty in the late nineteenth century. Japan's entry can be viewed, therefore, as a major stepping stone for further institutionalisation of the European system as it incorporated alien elements, contributing to its further complexity and adaptability by convincing the Europeans of the capability of non-European countries to develop to meet the European standard. Consequently, some countries in Asia emulated Japan's conforming behaviour. Thailand, for example, adopted the Japanese style of legal reform and educational system under the modernisation movement under the king.[41]

As was discussed previously, institutional adaptability is a process where an institution incorporates new elements that outside actors and major environmental changes bring. The international system has adapted and transformed itself while acquiring new institutional characteristics throughout modern history: the emergence of territorial states during the seventeenth century, the rise of an exclusively European concept of "standard of civilisation" during the nineteenth century, and the emergence of "negative sovereignty regime" in the twentieth century guaranteeing the legal equality of all members of international society. From a different angle, Japan's entry also marked the beginning of the transformation of the international system from nineteenth-century positivism to today's legal globalism. With the subsequent entrance of other non-European countries into the international system, the concept of national self-determination gradually emerged by the end of World War I and was manifested more explicitly by the decolonisation process after World War II. In this sense Japan's conformity to the "standard of civilisation" bridged the *de facto* sovereignty regime of the nineteenth century and the *de jure* sovereignty regime of the present,[42] producing certain institutional dynamics between "agents and structures," while international society obtained greater homogeneity in diplomatic intercourse and in its definition of sovereign statehood based on a legalistic definition of territory and international recognition. This homogeneity was the consequence of the globalising world, where some kind of objectivity needed to be created in defining statehood with increased heterogeneity in domestic characteristics of member states.

The expansion of Eurocentrism and the socialisation of the newcomer states were thus "synchronic" phenomena. What we see is the complicity between the socialisation of newcomers and institutional adaptation of the international system.[43] The Western concept of sovereignty, the European international system, and the "standard" were also reconstituted and reshaped through the addition of the newcomers. Whether imposed against the will, reluctantly accepted, or eagerly embraced,[44] the emergence of the "standard of civilisation" and newcomers' conformity to it contributed to the institutionalisation of the existing international system, strengthening its durability and autonomy.

7 Conclusion

During the wave of "new institutionalism" in the scholarship of comparative politics and IR since the 1990s, several important works on state building have appeared. Among them was Hendrik Spruyt's *The Sovereign State and Its Competitors*.[1] He explained how sovereign states emerged as the most efficient political entities in dealing with externalities by developing a nonlinear model of institutional selection. His insightful analysis emphasised the functional capabilities at which the state excelled vis-à-vis other political entities as an institution that worked as the causal mechanism of its emergence. An external logic of sovereignty, not just the domestic logic, however, demands attention in explaining the maintenance of the state-system and its survival. Not only the state, but also the system of states, needs to be treated as an institution in order to include the external logic of sovereignty in the analytical fomulation.

If Spruyt's *The Sovereign State and Its Competitors* depicts the origin of the contemporary state, the explanation for its adaptation to a further institutionalised international system will require a model of "The Sovereign State and Its Conformists," where not only the state but also the state system itself is considered as an institution that constrains the behaviour of latecomer states. In this sense, this study is not so much an antithesis to Spruyt as a sequel to the model of Western European sovereign statehood that he presented. It is also an elaboration of what Tilly mentioned about the external logic of statehood that latecomers face in their nation-building endeavours. Further, the study is to be a prologue to the "negative sovereignty game" in the latter half of the twentieth century. This other important transformation of the international system and ruling norms has been examined most thoroughly by the quasi-states argument elegantly represented by Robert Jackson.[2] His work offers an excellent "second-image reversed" explanation for the survival of contemporary statehood in the third world on the basis of the institutionalised nature of the "negative sovereignty regime."

The quasi-states argument posits that the notion of sovereignty has changed intrinsically since World War II, especially in the 1950s and 1960s with the birth of the new international norm of decolonisation and national self-determination that eradicated colonialism. The emergence of many states legally recognised as independent but without effective government is explained by the structural constraints of the international system. According to this view, international society, which was an exclusively European club of nations during the nineteenth century, became a worldwide democracy based on a legal, external sense of sovereignty, with non-European states constituting a larger part of the membership in the latter half of the twentieth century. The survival and membership of today's states now rely on the new institutional mechanism of international society, or the "negative sovereignty," and the stability of the external sense of sovereignty brought by it. The right of self-determination, international peace and security, inviolability of borders, and nonintervention all came to be recognised as significant "rules of the game" in today's international politics.[3] Stability of international borders and the concomitant stability of the external sense of sovereignty have become unprecedented characteristics of today's international system.

Although a classical sense of sovereignty shared among developed countries consists of both juridical and empirical statehood (positive sovereignty), many of today's developing countries possess only a simple juridical status without empirical content (negative sovereignty).[4] The rules of international politics changed from a "positive sovereignty game" to a "negative sovereignty game," enabling the former colonies and territories to be recognised as sovereign entities regardless of whether they fulfill the criteria of empirical statehood. The change in the norm of sovereignty brought newcomer states a strikingly different nation-building agenda. Since juridical sovereignty once achieved has become inalienable and since the norms came to prevent the political demise of even the most inviable of empirical states, many third-world states continue to exist without solving their domestic dimension of security, embedding the "third-world security predicament."[5]

In the experience of the Western European countries, an external threat was an incentive to state building.[6] Wars contributed to the increase in national coherence and the creation of loyal citizens to collaborate in state-building efforts in the case of European countries, thus solving the internal dimension of security first in their state building. In other words, the threat to security came from outside of the state in the experience of Europe, enhancing the degree of national coherence. The lack of a sufficient external threat or of interstate wars has meant the lack of incentives to solve the internal dimension of security, which has become the major problem for today's third world. That is not to say that European state building constitutes a successful, smooth model. It was in fact through a long, brutal process that European states came to enjoy their contemporary stability and prosperity. They could fortunately afford time and violence in building their states, as the international norm of the era allowed them to. Today's newcomer states cannot enjoy such a luxury any more. They are under pressure to achieve statehood peacefully and quickly. Violence and instability are constantly checked with vigilance by globalised international society through the rapid flow of increased information. In the experience of Asian states facing the positivist state-building norms, external threats existed, but in a way they could avoid to a considerable degree by meeting the European "standard of civilisation." The positivist international norms of the late nineteenth century demanded that the newcomers solve the internal dimension of statehood more intensively than their European predecessors did, quicker and with less violence.

State building is thus tied closely to the international norm that constrains and defines a country's mode of national development. Dividing the transforming concept of statehood into the above-mentioned three historical stages enables one to highlight the peculiar feature of the nineteenth-century criteria of membership in international society. It is distinguished from both the Westphalian criteria that preceded it and criteria based on "negative sovereignty" that followed it.

I have emphasised the systemic imperative that international society has placed on actors seeking membership, while the contributions made by historians in this field have mostly examined the subject from the perspective of either social movement or diplomatic history. This study has been an attempt to locate Japan and Asia in the transforming power relations in international politics, moving the analytical level from the state to the international and bringing the "structure" into our consciousness beyond what is visual. While part and parcel to Japan's entrance into international society were the existence of domestic infrastructures and the nation's leaders' long-term goals in directing the country by balancing the international and domestic constraints, exclusive attention to these domestic attributes is insufficient in explaining the country's socialisation. For a more complete picture, one needs to examine the international pressures that the country faced, which eventually defined the nature of Japanese sovereign statehood. Japan's vigorous adoption of international law that proceeded in parallel with rapid armament, and Japan's insistence on the abrogation of unequal treaties on the basis of equality that proceeded in parallel with its imposition of unequal treaties on other Asian countries, can be understood by examining the interactions and dynamics of domestic and international factors involved.

This study overlaps and relies on the insights of many, not fitting neatly into any one of the major IR theories. While this study was conducted with the basic premise of anarchy as the embedded feature of international politics, I have incorporated time- and space-contingent dimensions, making my stance in line with poststructuralism, structuration theory developed by Giddens, and state-building literature developed by Moore, Tilly and others, which I have already touched on. Further, my approach shares many theoretical elements with institutionalism, as the theme in this study centres around compliance and cooperative behaviour of states as rational actors. Moreover, when institutions are defined as broadly as to include the sovereign state system, they merge with the concept of "structure" as independent variables that indirectly produce certain states' behaviour. The sovereign state system that I treat as an institution in this study functions as an international structure or an environment in which states are influenced to act in socialised manners. As the concepts of "structure" and "institution" overlap, so do the concepts of norms and ideas with "structure" and "institutions," since they narrow choices of a state and perpetuate certain behavioural patterns.

The process of treaty revision, the evaluation of the Iwakura Mission, and the role of foreign pressures in the modernisation and national development of Japan still leave us with unanswered questions that necessitate further studies. As is typical of the state-building literature based on history, this study suffers from the small number of dependent variables and the difficulty of falsification. The findings in this study should, therefore, be extended to more thorough crosssectional studies on the entry of other non-European states into international society. Japan succeeded in lifting the extraterritoriality in 1899; Turkey in 1923; Thailand in 1939; and China in 1943. Comparison with these cases along with those of Ethiopia, Korea, the United States, Russia, and other latecomer states would increase the number of observations for more generality and be useful in enhancing our understanding of the dynamics of the newcomers' socialisation and the systemic logic.[7] In light of the criticism against the current literature on norm dynamics for ignoring the variation across microprocesses of the units' adoption of international norms,[8] endogenous sources of pronorm behaviours as well as their dynamics with exogenous factors need to be more clearly identified.

The story of Japan's socialisation with international society continued even after the abrogation of unequal treaties, which makes it difficult again to identify a clear-cut landmark of Japan's entrance into international society. Japan's achievement of full international legal rights in 1899 with the abrogation of extraterritoriality was followed by the 1902 Anglo-Japanese military alliance with both countries recognised on an equal basis, The Hague Conferences in 1899 and 1907, and victory in the Russo-Japanese War in 1905. On the other hand, events such as the 1895 Triple Intervention after the Sino-Japanese War and the denial of a racial equality clause in the League Covenant in 1919 to 1920 make it difficult for one to acknowledge the full membership in international society that was supposed to have been rightfully given to Japan.

Moreover, Japan's exertions during the process of entry into international society to bring the country's standard into line with the expectations of European powers and to demonstrate its willingness and ability to uphold international law in fact may have been the harbinger of Japan's later diplomatic course that followed the flamboyant Meiji Era. The scrupulous efforts that Japan made in complying with the "standards of civilisation" in order to obtain an equal status in international society made the country more sensitive to the treatment that it received from international society, eventually turning to frustrations and complaints against international society in early Showa. When the possibility of making peace was brought up for the first time during the Russo-Japanese War by a French initiative on March 1, 1905, for example, the Japanese chargé d'affaires in France, Motono Ichiro, was appalled at the proposal made by French foreign minister Theophile Delcasse that peace would be possible as long as Japan did not demand any territory or compensation.[9] Since it was the most proper European custom that a loser country pay compensation to the winner and give territories, he was shocked to realise how much Japan was looked down on by the West. By this time, Japan had already defeated the Russian fleet in Port Arthur and won the battles in Fengtien.[10] Moreover, Japan's faithful observance of wartime international law had been thoroughgoing during the Russo-Japanese War, showing its dedication to the principle of noninterference with the land or the property of the people in China, which became the battlefields for Japan and Russia, and offering every possible hospitality that a country could afford for Russian war prisoners. While it seemed obvious that, as the winner of the war, Japan would take compensation from Russia, the French proposal was to deny such a common European custom to an Asian newcomer. [11]

Further, on top of the prohibition against racial discrimination in the Covenant of the League of Nations that they appealed but failed, the Japanese were also dismayed at the rejection of the endorsement of the principle of the equality of nations and the just treatment of their nationals at the Paris Peace Conference after World War I despite a majority of eleven out of the seventeen states voting in favour. The US "Gentlemen's Agreement" in 1913, the California citizenship acts in 1917, and the anti-Japanese American Immigration Act in 1924, all of which discriminated against Japanese immigrants, also firmly engraved the unfair reality of international life in the minds of the Japanese.

Gong notes:

> Japan turned against the "civilized" Powers in part because it perceived itself to have struggled hard to join them, only to be denied a fair place after fulfilling the requirements set forth in their standard of "civilization." If anything, Japan took the standard too seriously and naively, on face value, not understanding that even "civilized" international society was characterised by anarchy (the absence of a monopoly of legitimate violence) and hierarchy (because without civil society, rights depend largely on might).[12]

The "standard of civilisation" thus eventually proved to be a double standard for Japan. When it came to understand that other civilised nations were disregarding the "standard" in their treatment of Japan despite its fulfillment of the requirement for the international membership, Japan left international society in the 1930s. The laborious dedication and sacrifice that Japan consecrated to the treaty revisions themselves had been the origins of Japanese imperialism in the 1930s. The norm of imperialism, which was the flip side of the "standard of civilisation," had also become out of date when Japan finally caught up with the West.[13]

By around World War I, worldwide international society gradually started to emerge; by decolonisation after World War II, international society had become truly global. With the decline of Europe, "the standard of civilisation" was no longer a standard for the membership in international society. The concept of nation states also changed. International society, which had displayed the highest degree of cultural and moralistic coherence based on the European standard at the time of Japan's entry, transformed itself today into one based on legal equality. The international recognition of states today is conducted according to the simple criteria of defined territory and population.

After the end of World War II, Japan faced another socialisation agenda of regaining its sovereignty after the US occupation and economic recovery from the devastation of war. Through the process of negotiation towards the San Francisco Peace Treaty, the leaders again demonstrated their capability to assess the international constraints, to evaluate national power, and to find congruity between them in directing the course of the country. The start of the Cold War further confirmed Japan's diplomatic course as a member of the capitalist "West" and laid foundations for what they call the postwar economic "miracle." The changes in the international environment brought by the end of the Cold War have been again demanding Japan to reassess its foreign policy vis-a-vis international society.

Since Meiji, Japan's foreign policy behaviour has often been described as an "anomaly," including its meteoric rise to modernisation and to great power status during Meiji, its deviation from the norms of international society in early Showa, its rapid economic recovery after World War II, which came to be gradually criticised as "free-riding" in accordance with Japan's further increase in economic power, and its low-key profile in international security that became the target of the normalcy debate.[14] Placed in perspective, however, Japan's foreign policy does not constitute an anomaly. Socialisation is the product of the systemic constraints, the isomorphic attributes of the country, and the capacity of national leaders who make them "hang together." While Japan's sedimented pacifism and exclusively defensive posture are often regarded as the major features of its abnormality today, consideration of what the post–World War II international norms expected for Japan and what Japanese leaders have faced domestically demystifies

Japan's behaviour. What is needed, in place of the autotoxemic view that emphasises Japan's uniqueness often supported by the Japanese themselves, is to "relativise" and place the country in the long-term and cross-sectional perspectives.

* * *

The positivist era was distinctive in history in a sense that rules and norms based on common culture are rather rarely observed in the history of international society. They are more often than not created by the recognition of common interests among states than by common culture. Today, the international system has adapted itself to a new international environment by transforming its rules of coexistence among states. International society has survived by adjusting itself to changes brought by new members, acquiring greater institutional autonomy and flexibility. While new rules of international society, such as the right of self-determination and human rights, emerged, behind these new norms of the twentieth and twenty-first centuries remain the basic European institutions and rules of international law, sovereignty, diplomatic procedures and customs, and international organisations that non-European countries have embraced since the nineteenth century and that have become firmly embedded.

Japan's continued struggle for recognition by international society proved to be another indication of the institutional forcefulness of the European international system that operates at a structural level. It was also an indication of the tension that existed between "autonomy" and "complexity" as criteria of institutionalisation of the international system. The Eurocentric international system preserved a certain level of "autonomy" and "coherence," while adapting itself to become a more complex, durable system by incorporating new elements brought by newcomers. Japan's entry brought unintended consequences to the institutionalisation of the international system as the non-Western country accommodated itself in the international environment dominated by the West.

The sovereign state system that originated in Europe is an institution that constrains the behaviour of its members and at the same time transforms itself by accommodating changes in its membership and environment. Since its inception, it transformed itself from a Christian international system to a Eurodominant one to a universal one based on legally equal states. The core elements of the system as an institution have remained, however. The survival of *de jure* sovereignty for more than 400 years since Westphalia in an environment of radically changing membership in international society, changing technologies, increased economic interdependence, improved military capabilities, and concomitant change in the power configurations among states, is truly notable.

> [There] remained not a single area of the world that was not – at least in theory – part of a state built upon the model of the modern European state and integrated into the all-encompassing international legal community. International law in the form in which it had originally been developed among the European states became a global law, which until now has incorporated only a few elements of extra-European origin.[15]

While *de facto* control of the state has differed in degree, "there has been no challenge to juridical sovereignty; that is, no effort to replace sovereign statehood with some other authority structure."[16] The autonomy of the system as an institution has been maintained, while the system obtained flexibility and complexity by integrating new members. This study examined the complex process of a country's socialisation into the sovereign state system, which involved a striking degree of conformity and contestation on the part of newcomers and institutionalisation of the norms of the international system. Both intrinsic and contextual aspects need to be taken into account in explaining newcomers' entry into the European state system. In his illuminating book on sovereignty, Stephen Krasner emphasised the frequency of violation of the sovereign state norm, calling it "organized hypocrisy."[17] But is violation more significant than observance of international norms? Persistence of the international norms of conformity furthered by the institutionalising tendency of the state system and the socialising tendency of the actors may be a more salient feature of international politics than the occasional violations.

Notes

Chapter 1

1 See, for example, Ferdinand de Saussure, *Course in General Linguistics*, trans. Roy Harris (Chicago and La Salle: Open Court, 1972); Claude Levi-Strauss, *Structural Anthropology* (New York: Basic Books, 1963).

2 Included in this school are, for example, Wight's historical sociology, Bull's notions on order and society in international politics, and Vincent's prescriptions for a redistribution of wealth. Martin Wight, *International Theory: The Three Traditions* (London: Leicester University Press, 1991); *Power Politics* (London: Leicester University Press, 1978); *Systems of States* (London: Leicester University Press, 1977); Hedley Bull, *Anarchical Society: A Study of Order in World Politics* (London: MacMillan, 1977); Herbert Butterfield and Martin Wight, *Diplomatic Investigations: Essays in the Theory of International Politics* (London: George Allen & Unwin, 1966); R. J. Vincent and J.D.B. Miller, *Order and Violence: Hedley Bull and International Relations* (Oxford: Clarendon Press, 1990). For a comprehensive overview of the development of the English school, see Time Dunne, *Inventing International Society: A History of the English School* (Oxford: Macmillan, 1998).

3 See, for example, Douglass C. North and Robert Paul Thomas, *The Rise of the Western World: A New Economic History* (Cambridge: Cambridge University Press, 1973); Douglass C. North, *Structure and Change in Economic History* (New York: Norton & Company, 1981); Douglass C. North, *Institutions, Institutional Change and Economic Performance* (Cambridge: Cambridge University Press, 1990).

4 As an example of treating the international system as an institution, see Stephen Krasner, "Westphalia and All That," in *Ideas and Foreign Policy:*

Beliefs, Institutions, and Political Change, ed. Judith Goldstein and Robert O. Keohane (Ithaca, NY: Cornell University Press, 1990).

5 Some of the excellent works on the subject with political science implications include, for example, Barrington Moore Jr., *Social Origins of Dictatorship and Democracy: Lord and Peasant in the Making of the Modern World* (Boston: Beacon Press, 1966); Ellen Kay Trimberger, *Revolution from Above: Military Bureaucrats and Development in Japan, Turkey, Egypt, and Peru* (New Brunswick, NJ: Transaction Books, 1978).

6 Lydia Liu, "Desire for the Sovereign and the Logic of Reciprocity in the Family of Nations," *Diacritics* 29, no. 4 (Winter 1999): 151.

7 Gerrit Gong, *The Standard of "Civilization" in International Society* (Oxford: Clarendon Press, 1984).

8 The terms are used by John Peter Stern. See *The Japanese Interpretation of the "Law of Nations," 1854–1874* (Princeton, NJ: Princeton University Press, 1979).

9 Thucydides, *History of the Peloponnesian War* (Book 5:89) (London: Penguin Classics, 1972).

10 Most of the standard history textbooks explain the reasons for Japan's opening up of the nation this way. See, for example, Matsusada Inoue et al., *Shōsetsu Nihonshi* [Detailed Japanese History] (Tokyo: Yamakawa, 1993).

11 Kenneth N. Waltz, *Theory of International Politics* (New York: McGraw-Hill, 1979).

12 Ibid., ch. 4.

13 Ibid.

14 One recent school of international relations that seeks to revive liberalism (distinguished from the neoliberal institutionalism that led the liberal school in the 1980s and early 1990s) asserts that domestic attributes should not be treated as residues. This school argues that, instead of starting with systemic factors and going down to the domestic level later, we should always start with domestic attributes. See, for example, Andrew Moravcsik, "Taking Preferences Seriously: A Liberal Theory of International Politics," *International Organizations* 51, no. 4 (Autumn 1997): 513–53; Andrew Moravcsik, "Introduction: Integrating International and Domestic Theories of International Bargaining," in *Double-Edged Diplomacy: International Barganing and Domestic Politics*, ed., Peter B. Evans, Harold K. Jacobson, and Robert D. Putnam (Berkeley: University of California Press, 1993), ch. 1; Helen V. Milner, *Interests, Institutions, and Information: Domestic Politics and International Relations* (Princeton, NJ: Princeton University Press, 1997). My position is that starting with domestic attributes could give researchers an

incorrect orientation of the study, frustrating the coherence of empirical knowledge, especially in conducting research that deals with a long historical time span.

15 Charles Tilly, "Reflections on the History of European State-Making," in *The Formation of National States in Western Europe,* ed. Charles Tilly (Princeton, NJ: Princeton University Press, 1975), 84–163.

16 Alexander Gerschenkron, *Economic Backwardness in Historical Perspective* (Cambridge, MA: Harvard University Press, 1962); Albert Hirschman, *A Bias for Hope* (New Haven, CT: Yale University Press, 1971). Barrington Moore's *Social Origin of Dictatorship and Democracy* also offers a perspective on time-contingent routes to different social systems. See also Thorstein Veblen, "The Opportunity of Japan," *The Journal of Race Development* 6, no. 1 (July 1915): 23–38.

17 Robert H. Jackson and Carl Rosberg, "Why Africa's Weak States Persist: The Empirical and Juridical in Statehood," *World Politics* 35, no. 1 (1982): 1–24; Robert H. Jackson, *Quasi-states: Sovereignty, International Relations, and the Third World* (Cambridge: Cambridge University Press, 1993).

18 Reference to time lag also often appears in standard textbooks on Japanese history.

19 Japan learned about China's defeat in the Opium War through Nagasaki and Ryūkyū (today's Okinawa Prefecture). A shogunate leader, Abe, immediately delivered the news to all the major feudal nobles. Motegi Toshio, *Henyōsuru Kindai Higashiajia no Kokusaichitsujo* [Transforming International Order of Modern East Asia] (Tokyo: Yamakawa, 2004), 41.

20 On Thailand's entry into international society, see Gong, *The Standard of "Civilization,"* ch. 7.

21 The attitude of tending to learn from abroad is said to have traditionally existed in Japan, starting with the missions sent to China in the seventh and eighth centuries. Not only were the plans of Japan's former capital cities and its governmental institutions patterned on China, the Japanese written language itself was also an import from there.

22 John K. Fairbank, Edwin O. Reischauer, and Albert M. Craig, *East Asia: The Modern Transformation* (Boston: Houghton Mifflin Company, 1965), 189.

23 Ibid., 180–81.

24 Ibid., 189.

25 See, for example, the classic description of this aspect of the Japanese by Ruth Benedict, *The Chrysanthemum and the Sword* (Boston: Houghton Mifflin, 1946).

26 This term is often associated with the work of the World Polity Perspective in Sociology represented by John Meyer and others, who have examined

the macrohistorical spread of norms and social practices such as sovereignty, market economies, and rationalism. They use the term as something that spread as actors accept international norms and practices. See John W. Meyer, John Boli, George M. Thomas, and Francisco Ramirez, "World Society and the Nation-State," *American Journal of Sociology* 103, no. 1 (July 1997): 144–81; David Strang, "From Dependency to Sovereignty: An Event History Analysis of Decolonization 1870–1987," *American Sociological Review* 55, no. 6 (December 1990): 846–60; Didem Buhart-Gulmez, "Stanford School on Sociological Institutionalism: A Global and Cultural Approach," *International Political Sociology* 4, no. 3 (September 2010): 253–70. "Isomorphism" is used here to mean the functional equivalents of institutions in a country that are different in outlook, but play the same roles and functions in the society, facilitating international actors to accommodate themselves to the macrosocietal norms of international relations.

27 Tadao Umesao, *Bunmei no Seitaishi Kan* [An Ecological View of History] (Tokyo: Chūō Kōron Sha, 1967). It is also published in English as *An Ecological View of History: Japanese Civilization in the World Context* (International Specialized Book Service, 2003). His other works published in English include "Japan as Viewed from an Eco-Historical Perspective," *Review of Japanese Culture and Society* 1, no. 1 (1986): 25–31, and "Introduction to an Ecological View of Civilization," *Japan Echo* 22 (Special Issue, 1995): 42–50.

28 Although elements of geopolitical landmass versus peripheral island may be noticeable in Umesao's arguments, his intention was rather to challenge Arnold Toynbee's theory of civilisation based on an analogy of a life cycle. A. J. Toynbee, *A Study of History* (London: Oxford University Press, 1946).

29 Umesao does mention that, due to Japan's peculiar policy of closing the country, the nation's feudal collapse and colonial expansion were delayed by 200 years, postponing the accumulation of wealth. Umesao, *Bunmei no Seitaishi Kan*.

30 The feudal system is generally said to eventually awaken people's sense of the individual "self" by nurturing the bourgeois class that initiates revolutions, which leads to highly developed industrial societies.

31 In contrast, Umesao describes the history of inland areas as a cyclical rise and fall of great empires, where nomads have been the sources of destruction and conquest. Most of the countries in the inland areas used to be colonies or half-colonies; capitalism remains immature in these areas. In ancient history, the high standard of civilisation in the inland areas had no comparison in the coastal areas. Revolutions in these areas, however, led to authoritarian political systems. Feudalism did not precede revolutions,

but authoritarian monarchy or colonial rule, which could never be a fertile ground to raise the bourgeois. Enormous empires such as the tsarist system in Russia, the Qing Dynasty in China, the Mugal Empire, and the Turkish Empire share many social phenomena in parallel: extravagant castles and courts, vast land, complicated ethnic structure, existence of periphery and satellites, poverty and ignorance of farmers, major landlords, corruption, and collapse.

32 Umesao, *Bunmei no Seitaishi Kan.*

33 Yoshihiko Amino, *Nihon no Rekishi wo Yominaosu II* (Tokyo: Chikuma Shobo, 1996) 8–49. Its English translation, *Rethinking Japanese History,* was just published by the Center for Japanese Studies, the University of Michigan (Michigan Monograph Series in Japanese Studies, No. 74, Ann Arbor, 2012).

34 Fairbanks, Reischauer, and Craig, *East Asia*, 191. For analyses of economic development, see also William Lockwood, *The Economic Development of Japan: Growth and Structural Change, 1868–1938* (Princeton, NJ: Princeton University Press, 1954); Henry Rosovsky, *Capital Formation in Japan* (Glencoe: Free Press, 1961); Johannes Hirschmeier, *The Origins of Entrepreneurship in Meiji Japan* (Cambridge, MA: Harvard University Press, 1964); Hayami Akira, Saito Osamu, and Ronald P. Toby, *Emergence of Economic Society in Japan, 1600–1859* (Oxford: Oxford University Press, 2004).

35 Studies on these institutions that had existed since premodern Japan originated in the works of John Hall and Marius Jansen. See John W. Hall and Marius Jansen, *Studies in the Institutional History of Early Modern Japan* (Princeton, NJ: Princeton University Press, 1970) and John W. Hall, *Japanese History: New Dimensions of Approach and Understanding* (Washington, D.C.: Service Center for Teachers of History, 1961). For recent works, see, for example, Mary Elizabeth Berry, *Japan in Print: Information and Nation in the Early Modern Period* (Berkeley: University of California Press, 2006); Daniel V. Botzman, *Punishment and Power in the Making of Modern Japan* (Princeton, NJ: Princeton University Press, 2005); Penelope Francks, *The Japanese Consumer: An Alternative Economic History of Modern Japan* (Cambridge: Cambridge University Press, 2009).

36 Fairbanks, Reischauer, and Craig mention that "in China, by contrast, though the top level of administrative organization under the emperor was more centralized, loyalties even within the bureaucracy were more diffuse; obligations to family or to local community competed with duty to emperor and to society" (*East Asia,* 181).

37 Ibid., 193.

38 Hendrik Spruyt, *The Sovereign State and Its Competitors* (Princeton, NJ: Princeton University Press, 1994); Charles Tilly, *Coercion, Capital, and European States: AD 990–1990* (Cambridge: Blackwell, 1990); Tilly, "Reflections on the History"; North and Thomas, *The Rise of the Western World;* North, *Structure and Change.*

39 See, for example, Thomas Bartlett, *The Making of Europe: Conquest, Colonization, and Cultural Change* (Princeton, NJ: Princeton University Press, 1993); Thomas Ertman, *Birth of the Leviathan: Building States and Regimes in Medieval and Early Modern Europe* (Cambridge: Cambridge University Press, 1997); Michael Howard, *War in European History* (Oxford: Oxford University Press, 1976); Bernard S. Silberman, *Cages of Reason: The Rise of the Rational State in France, Japan, the United States, and Great Britain* (Chicago: University of Chicago Press, 1992); Spruyt, *The Sovereign State;* Hendrik Spruyt, "Institutional Selection in International Relations: State Anarchy as Order," *International Organization* 48 (Autumn 1994): 527–57; Charles Tilly, "War-making and State-making as Organised Crime," in *Bringing the State Back In,* ed. Evans, Rueschemeyer, and Skocpol (Cambridge: Cambridge University Press, 1985), 169–91; Tilly, "Reflections on the History"; Tilly, *Coercion.*

40 Skeptical views on economic interdependence and globalisation are presented, for example, in Paul Hirst and G. Thompson, *Globalization in Question* (Cambridge: Cambridge University Press, 1996); Chris Brown, "International Political Theory and the Idea of World Community," *International Relations Theory Today,* ed. Ken Booth and Steve Smith (University Park: The Pennsylvania State University Press, 1995) 90–109.

41 British scholars Buzan and Little, for example, consider the linkage between IR and history as "an essential act" for IR scholarship to develop as a social science. Barry Buzan and Richard Little, *International Systems in World History: Remaking the Study of International Relations* (Oxford: Oxford University Press, 2000), 385.

42 See, for example, Anne-Marie Slaughter, Andrew S. Tulumello, and Stepan Wood, "International Law and International Relations Theory: A New Generation of Interdisciplinary Scholarship," *American Journal of International Law* 92, no. 3 (1998): 367–97; Anne-Marie Slaughter, "International Law and International Relations Theory: A Dual Agenda," *American Journal of International Law* 87 (1993); Friedrich V. Kratochwill, *Rules, Norms, and Decisions: On the Conditions of Practical and Legal Reasoning in International and Domestic Affairs* (Cambridge: Cambridge University Press, 1989); Nicholas Onuf, *World of Our Making: Rules and Rule in Social Theory and International Relations* (Columbia: University of South Carolina Press, 1989).

43 The interdisciplinary tensions and opportunities for collabouration are fully discussed in Colin Elman and Mariam Fendius Elman, eds., *Bridges and Boundaries: Historians, Political Scientists, and the Study of International Relations* (Cambridge, MA: MIT Press, 2001); *International Security* 22, no. 1 (Summer 1997); Christopher Hill, "History and International Relations," in *International Relations: British and American Perspectives,* ed. Steve Smith (Oxford: Basil Blackwell, 1985); Gordon Craig, "Historian and the Study of International Relations," *American Historical Review* 9, no. 1 (February 1983); Clayton Roberts, *The Logic of Historical Explanation* (University Park: Pennsylvania State University Press, 1996); Barry Buzan and Richard Little, "The Idea of 'International System': Theory Meets History," *International Political Science Review* 15, no. 3 (1994): 231–55; Buzan and Little, "Reconceptualising Anarchy: Structural Realism Meets World History," *European Journal of International Relations* 2, no. 4 (1996): 403–38.

44 A good example of political scientists' use of history is Machiavelli's *Discourses on Livy,* where he used Livy's Roman history to support his political views. The treatment of the rise and fall of great powers from the perspective of the interaction between national wealth and military strategy by Paul Kennedy is another example. Niccolò Machiavelli, *Discourses on Livy* (Oxford: Oxford University Press, 1997); Paul M. Kennedy, *The Rise and Fall of the Great Powers: Economic Change and Military Conflict from 1500 to 2000* (New York: Random House, 1987).

45 The debate was triggered by an article by the Japanese politician, Ichiro Ozawa, "Futsūno no Kuni ni Nare [Become a Normal Country]," *Sengo Nihon Gaikō Ronshū [Postwar Japanese Diplomatic Writings]*, ed. Shin'ichi Kitaoka (Tokyo: Chūō Kōron Sha, 1995): 461–81. On recent discussions on Japan's normalcy, see Andrew L. Oros, *Normalizing Japan: Politics, Identity, and the Evolution of Security Practice* (Stanford, CA: Stanford University Press, 2008); Yoshihide Soeya, Masayuki Tadokoro, and David A. Welch, eds., *Japan as a Normal Country?* (Toronto: University of Toronto Press, 2011).

46 For discussions on the value of single-case studies, see, for example, Alexander L. George and Andrew Bennett, *Case Studies and Theory Development in the Social Sciences* (Cambridge, MA: MIT Press, 2005) 32–33, 80.

47 Alexander E. Wendt, "The Agent-Structure Problem in International Relations Theory," *International Organization* 41, no. 3 (Summer 1987); Colin Wight, *Agents, Structures and International Relations: Politics of Ontology* (New York: Cambridge University Press, 2006).

48 Japan was engaged in all three of these manifestations of international law; that is, international law as treatises, international norms, and treaties,

throughout the process of its entry into international society, although I tend to highlight one of these aspects in each historical period. The general texts of the law of nations, which were first introduced in 1860s, for example, continued to be studied by the Japanese with different versions of translations appearing one after another in the later period, especially the 1880s and 1890s. Likewise, revising unequal treaties had continually been the foremost concern of the Japanese leaders since the earlier period, although we had to wait until the 1890s for the amendment to materialise.

49 Depending on what aspects of statehood are to be focused on, it is plausible to treat other landmarks of recognition as an independent state. The abolition of tariff autonomy in 1911, for example, was actually the final removal of all the unequal treaties that Japan had concluded. The victory in the Russo-Japanese War in 1905 can be also considered an important turning point, as it enabled Japan to join the great powers. As another perspective, the Correlates of War (COW) project measures a country's entry into the international system by diplomatic recognition by either Britain or France until 1919 and by membership in the League of Nations or the United Nations after 1919. The importance of the abrogation of extraterritoriality lies in the fact that it concerns the territorial integrity of a nation, which is fundamental to modern statehood, and therefore, strongly appealed to the Japanese public as a symbol of national pride. It also affected the later course of Japanese history by increasing the level of national coherence and mobility.

Chapter 2

1 Samuel Huntington, *Political Order in Changing Societies* (New Haven, CT: Yale University Press, 1968). The discussions and theories on institutionalisation have been integrated into the study of institutional change and regime/norm transformation. Elements in Huntington's institutionalisation can be still observed in, for example, Stephen Haggard and Beth Simmons, "Theories of International Regimes," *International Organization* 41 (1987): 481–517; Judith L. Goldstein, Miles Kahler, Robert O. Keohane, and Anne-Marie Slaughter, *Legalization and World Politics* (Cambridge, MA: MIT Press, 2001).

2 P. E. Freedman and A. Freedman, "Political Learning," in *The Handbook of Political Behavior*, vol. 1, ed. S. Long (New York: Plenum Press, 1981), 258; O. Ichilov, ed., *Political Socialization, Citizenship Education and Democracy* (New York: Teachers College Press, 1990), 1–8; See also, Gabriel Almond

and James Coleman, eds., *The Politics of Developing Areas* (Princeton, NJ: Princeton University Press, 1960), 26–58.

3 S. Stryker and A. Statham, "Symbolic Interaction and Role Theory," in *The Handbook of Social Psychology,* vol. 1, ed. G. Lindzey and E. Aronson (New York: Random House, 1985), 325.

4 The treatment of states as units is discussed, for example, in Kenneth N. Waltz, *Man, the State, and War* (New York: Columbia University Press, 1954), 172–80. Bull's discussions on "international order" versus "world order" are also helpful. Hedley Bull, *The Anarchical Society: A Study of Order in World Politics* (London: MacMillan, 1977), 20–22.

5 G. John Ikenberry and Charles A. Kupchan, "Socialization and Hegemonic Power," *International Organization* 44, no. 3 (Summer 1990): 284, 289–90.

6 For a systematic treatment of this process, see, for example, Robert D. Putnam, "Diplomacy and Domestic Politics: The Logic of Two-Level Games," *International Organization* 42, no. 3 (Summer 1988): 427–60; Peter E. Evans, Harold K. Jacobson, and Robert D. Putnam, *Double-Edged Diplomacy: International Bargaining and Domestic Politics* (Berkeley: University of California Press 1993).

7 See, for example, Abram Chayes and Antonia Handler Chayes, "On Compliance," *International Organization* 47 (Spring, 1993): 175–206; Martha Finnemore and Kathryn Sikkink, "International Norm Dynamics and Political Change," *International Organization* 52, no. 4 (Autumn 1998): 887–917.

8 Scholars of the English school in fact differ in the degree to which they treat interstate relations as a society. Claire A. Cutler distinguishes the differences between Grotian and neo-Grotian views as "solidalist" versus "pluralist." Claire A. Cutler, "Grotian Tradition in International Relations," *Review of International Studies* 17 (1991): 41–65. Bull is placed in the pluralist, neo-Grotian category, which exhibits more theoretical affinity to realism than the solidarists.

9 Bull, *Anarchical Society,* ch. 6.

10 Ibid., 140.

11 Robert O. Keohane, "Neoliberal Institutionalism: A Perspective on World Politics, " in *International Institutions and State Power: Essays in International Relations Theory,* ed. Robert O. Keohane (Boulder: Westview, 1989), 1–20.

12 Ibid. Another comprehensive and explicit statement of neoliberal institutionalism is contained in Robert O. Keohane, *After Hegemony: Cooperation and Discord in the World Political Economy* (Princeton, NJ: Princeton University Press, 1986); and "International Institutions: Two Approaches," *International Studies Quarterly* 32 (1988): 379–96.

13 Stephen D. Krasner, "State Power and the Structure of International Trade," *World Politics* 28 (April 1976): 317–47.
14 Waltz, *Theory of International Politics*, 75–76.
15 Ibid., 77.
16 For a discussion on neorealist ideas of socialisation, see, for example, Cameron G. Thies, "State Socialization and Structural Realism," *Security Studies* 19 (2010): 689–717.
17 Alexander Wendt, *Social Theory of International Politics* (Cambridge: Cambridge University Press, 1999); and "Collective Identity Formation and the International State," *American Political Science Review* 88 (1999): 384–96.
18 Alastair Iain Johnston, *Social States: China in International Institutions, 1980–2000* (Princeton, NJ: Princeton University Press, 2008), xv.
19 Finnemore and Sikkink, "International Norm Dynamics"; Amitav Acharya, "How Ideas Spread: Whose Norms Matter? Norm Localization and Institutional Change in Asian Regionalism," *International Organization* 58 (2004): 239–75.
20 While the term "imperative" is often associated with neorealism and the term "incentive" with institutionalism, the distinction between them is often blurred. State survival, for example, can be both an imperative and an incentive that take the form of socialization and competition. Both imperatives and incentives embed actors' conforming behaviour.
21 Kai Alderson, "Making Sense of State Socialisation," *Review of International Studies* 27 (2001): 415–33.
22 Ibid.
23 Finnemore and Sikkink, "International Norm Dynamics." See also the spiral models of norm internalisation of Trin Flockhart, "Complex Socialization: A Framework for the Study of State Socialization," *European Journal of International Relations* 12: 89–118; and Thomas Risse-Kappen, Steve C. Ropp, and Kathryn Sikkink, *The Power of Human Rights: Internatlonal Norms and Domestic Change* (Cambridge: Cambridge University Press, 1999).
24 Johnston, *Social States*. See also Alastair Iain Johnston, "Treating International Institutions as Social Environments," *International Studies Quarterly* 45 (2001): 487–515.
25 Related to this theme are some of the recent studies on European integration that focus on state socialisation in highly institutionalised international environments. Jeffrey T. Checkel, "International Institutions and Socialization in Europe: Introduction and Framework," *International Organization* 59 (Fall 2005): 801–26; Trine Flockhart, "Masters and Novices: Socialization and Social Learning through the NATO Parliamentary Assembly," *International Relations* 18 (September 2004): 361–80; and Frank

Schimmelofennig, "International Socialization in the New Europe: Rational Action in an Institutional Environment," *European Journal of International Relations* 6 (March 2000): 109–39.

26 Major contributions of North include North and Thomas, *The Rise of the Western World;* North, *Structure and Change;* and *Institutions and Institutional Change.*

27 See, for example, Spruyt, *The Sovereign State;* and "Institutional Selection"; Tilly, *Coercion.*

28 North, *Structure and Change,* 201–2. In North's *Institutions and Institutional Change,* they are defined as "the rules of the game in a society, the human-devised constraints that shape human interaction."

29 James March and Johan P. Olsen, "The Institutional Dynamics of International Political Orders," *International Organization* 52, no. 4 (Autumn 1998): 943–69; March and Olsen, "The New Institutionalism: Organizational Factors in Political Life," *American Political Science Review* 78, no. 3 (September 1984): 734–49; March and Olsen, *Rediscovering Institutions* (New York: Free Press, 1989).

30 William H. Riker, "Implications from the Disequilibrium of Majority Rule for the Study of Institutions," *American Political Science Review* 74 (June 1980): 444–45.

31 Defining international institutions as "explicit rules, agreed upon by governments, which pertain to particular sets of issues in international relations," R. O. Keohane categorises institutionalism into two groups: "rationalistic theory," which focuses on specific institutions as "a particular human-constructed arrangement," and the "sociological approach," which emphasises the role of underlying practices including culture, norms, and value systems influencing the formation of persistent social forces that constrain and prescribe actors' behaviour and expectations. Robert O. Keohane, "Neoliberal Institutionalism: A Perspective on World Politics," in *International Institutions and State Power: Essays in International Relations Theory,* ed. Robert O. Keohane (Boulder: Westview Press, 1989), 1–20; Keohane, "International Institutions," 195.

32 Steinmo and Thelen note the necessity of "explicit theorizing on the reciprocal influence of institutional constraints and political strategies" that reflect how ideas, interests and institutions interact. Sven Steinmo and Kathleen Thelen, "Historical Institutionalism in Comparative Politics," in *Structuring Politics: Historical Institutionalism in Comparative Analysis,* ed. Sven Steinmo, Kathleen Thelen, and Frank Longstreth (Cambridge: Cambridge University Press, 1992), 14; Kathleen Thelen, "Historical Institutionalism in Comparative Politics," *Annual Review of Political Science* 2 (1999): 369–404.

33 Terry Nardin, "International Pluralism and the Rule of Law," *Review of International Studies* 26 (December 2000): 96.
34 K. J. Holsti, "Scholarship in an Era of Anxiety: The Study of International Politics During the Cold War," in *The Eighty Years' Crisis: International Relations 1919–1999,* ed. Tim Dunne, Michael Cox, and Ken Booth (Cambridge: Cambridge University Press, 1998), 17–46.
35 Edward H. Carr, *The Twenty Years' Crisis, 1919–1939: An Introduction to the Study of International Relations* (New York: Harper & Row, 1964), 177–78.
36 Bull, *Anarchical Society,* 140; Keohane, *After Hegemony;* and "International Institutions."
37 Huntington, *Political Order,* 12.
38 Ibid., 12–23.
39 Ibid., 22.
40 Stephen D. Krasner, *Sovereignty: Organised Hypocrisy* (Princeton, NJ: Princeton University Press, 1999), 58.
41 As is well known, countries and regions such as China, India, and Assyria developed their own codes of interstate relations in ancient times. They have no connection to the current codes of modern international relations since Westphalia, however. See, for example, R. P. Anand, "Attitude of the Asian-African Countries toward Certain Problems of International Law," *International Comparative Law Quarterly* 15 (1966): 57.
42 Jörg Fisch, "The Role of International Law in the Territorial Expansion of Europe, 16th–20th Centuries," *ICCLP Review* 3, no.1 (March, 2000): 5–15.
43 See, for example, Spruyt, *The Sovereign State;* Tilly, *Coercion;* Bartlett, *The Making of Europe;* Ertman, *Birth of Leviathan.*
44 Tilly, in fact, periodises the history of the state with three marking points: 990, 1490, and 1990. Tilly, *Coercion.*
45 Tilly, "Reflections on the History."
46 Gould's theory of punctuated equilibrium states that a rapid evolutionary change occurs after long periods of stasis, arguing against the Darwinian theory of gradual evolution. Stephen Jay Gould and Niles Eldredge, "Punctuated Equilibria: An Alternative to Phyletic Gradualism," in *Models in Paleobiology,* ed. T.J.M. Schopf (San Francisco: Freeman, Cooper and Company, 1972), 82–115.
47 Spruyt, *The Sovereign States;* and "Institutional Selection."
48 Duncan Bell, ed., *Victorian Vision of Global Order: Empire and International Relations in Nineteenth-Century Political Thought* (Cambridge: Cambridge University Press, 2007).
49 Alexis Dudden, "Japan's Engagement with International Terms," in *Tokens of Exchange: The Problem of Translation in Global Circulations,* ed. Lydia H. Liu (Durham, NC: Duke University Press, 1999), 168.

50 Paul W. Schroeder, *The Transformation of European Politics, 1763–1848* (Oxford: Clarendon, 1996).

51 Adam Watson, *The Evolution of International Society* (New York: Routledge, 1992).

52 Carr, *The Twenty Years' Crisis*, 176.

53 Anthony Anghie, "Finding the Peripheries: Sovereignty and Colonialism in Nineteenth-Century International Law," *Harvard International Law Journal* 40 (Winter 1999): 2.

54 Kayaoğlu explains the extraterritorial arrangements of Japan, the Ottoman Empire, and China from the perspective of the new legal framework of positivism in the era of Western imperialism, which imposed the adoption of specific domestic legal reforms on Asian countries. Turan Kayaoğlu, *Legal Imperialism: Sovereignty and Extraterritoriality in Japan, the Ottoman Empire, and China* (New York: Cambridge University Press, 2010).

55 Bull notes that natural law had mitigated the exclusiveness of the idea of Christian international society by emphasising universal rights and duties of all men. "In the era of European international society, the decline of natural-law thinking withdrew this mitigating influence." Bull, *Anarchical Society*, 34.

56 Carr, *The Twenty Years' Crisis*, 176. Positivist turn can be also interpreted from different perspectives. Kayaoğlu, for example, observes this turn from a constructivist and postcolonial point of view. Kayaoğlu, *Legal Imperialism.*

57 Jean Bodin, *On Sovereignty: Four Chapters from the Six Books of the Commonwealth* (Cambridge: Cambridge University Press, 1992); Thomas Hobbes, *Leviathan* (London: Penguin Books, 1988).

58 As a major participant in the Crimean War, Turkey's presence was a prerequisite to end the war. At the Peace Conference in Paris in 1856 after the war, therefore, France, Austria, Britain, Prussia, and Russia along with Sardinia explicitly recognised Turkey's eligibility in the Concert of Europe and started to invite Turkey to all the major international conferences. It was not until the 1923 Treaty of Lausanne, however, that Turkey's extraterritoriality was lifted. Participation in international conferences constitutes an important but only one aspect of equal international membership.

59 Gong, *The Standard of "Civilization,"* 14–21.

60 Anghie, "Finding the Peripheries," 26–27.

61 Ibid. Anghie cites Oppenheim's argument that "European states interacted with non-European states on the basis of discretion, and not international law. The matter is resolved not in accordance with these detailed and elaborate principles, but rather on an almost completely ad hoc basis."

62 Anghie, "Finding the Peripheries," 43.
63 Gong, *The Standard of "Civilization."*

Chapter 3

1 On the unavoidable tension between periodisation and continuity of history, see, for example, Barry Buzan and Richard Little, *International Systems in World History: Remaking the Study of International Relations* (Oxford: Oxford University Press, 2000), 387.
2 "*Bakufu*" refers to the political authority during this time. It can also be translated simply as "government."
3 Kang investigates the nature of the Chinese tribute system that lasted from 1368 to 1841 as an international society based on culture, different from the Western international system featuring polarity. In his emphasis on the centrality of China in the East Asian system, he considers Japan's historical involvement in and borrowing from the Chinese system heavier than usually thought. David C. Kang, "Hierarchy and Legitimacy in International Systems: The Tribute System in Early East Asia," *Security Studies* 19 (2010): 591–622.
4 The former name of today's Okinawa Prefecture in Japan, used until 1879.
5 For further studies on the operation of the China-centered system, see, for example, Takeshi Hamashita, *Kindai Chūgoku no Kokusaiteki Keiki* [International Factors in Modern China] (Tokyo:University of Tokyo Press, 1990); Toshikazu Hori, *Chūgoku to Kodai Higashiajiasekai* [China and the Ancient East Asian World] (Tokyo: Iwanami, 1993).
6 Fisch notes that the Europeans "were fairly (although not completely) successful in America and, from the late nineteenth century, in Africa, but much less so in Asia," often failing to receive equal legal recognition from their local leaders. Fisch, "The Role of International Law," 7.
7 Anand, "Attitude of the Asian-African Countries," 58.
8 Fisch, "The Role of International Law," 7.
9 Anghie, "Finding the Peripheries," 17.
10 C. H. Alexandrowicz, "Mogul Sovereignty and the Law of Nations," *Indian Yearbook of International Affairs* 33 (1955): 317; Anand, "Attitudes of the Asian-African," 58.
11 Anand, "Attitudes of the Asian-African Countries," 59.
12 Fairbank, Reischauer, and Craig, *East Asia*, 180–81.
13 The message was delivered on December 6, 1852. J. D. Richardson, *Messages and Papers of the Presidents*, V, 167–68, cited in F. C. Jones, *Extraterritoriality in Japan and the Diplomatic Relations Resulting in Its Abolition, 1853–1899* (New Haven, CT: Yale University Press, 1931), 7.

14 John Bassett Moore, *A Digest of International Law*, V, 737, cited in Jones, *Extraterritoriality*, 8.
15 As an example, Japan fought the Mongolian invasions under Kublai Khan in 1274 and 1281 and successfully defended the country, helped by the typhoons that destroyed the Mongolian fleet and forced them to retreat.
16 Among them, for example, are the records by Luis Frois, Pero Diez, and Jorge Alvarez. The Blum Collection of the Yokohama Archives of History possesses numerous books and personal records by foreign visitors to Japan since the early period.
17 Jean Crasset, *Histoire de l'eglise du Japon* (Paris: Chez Estienne Michallet, 1689). It was published in Japanese, titled *Nihon Seikyōshi*, by several publishers after the Meiji government translated it.
18 For Satow's account of Japan, see Ernest Mason Satow, *A Diplomat in Japan* (Oxford: Oxford University Press, 1968).
19 Marius B. Jansen, *The Making of Modern Japan* (Cambridge, MA: Harvard University Press, 2000), 276.
20 For more about Abe, see, for example, Harold Bolitho, "Abe Masahiro and the New Japan," in *The Bakufu in Japanese History*, ed. Jeffrey P. Mass and William B. Hauser (Stanford, CA: Stanford University Press, 1985); Conrad Totman, "Political Reconciliation in the Tokugawa Bakufu: Abe Masahiro and Tokugawa Nariaki, 1844–1852," in *Personality in Japanese History*, ed. Albert Craig and Donald Howard Shively (Berkeley: University of California Press, 1970); Shujiro Watanabe, *Abe Masahiro Jiseki* [Deputy Abe Masahiro] (Tokyo: Tokyo Daigaku Shuppan-kai, 1978).
21 Interestingly, from about this time, information gathering and selling became a business in Japan. Sellers of information to *bakufu* officials and the general public, such as Fujioka-ya, appeared.
22 Fairbank, Reischauer, and Craig, *East Asia*, 182.
23 Gong, *The Standard of "Civilization,"* 170.
24 Jones, *Extraterritoriality*, 1.
25 Stephen Krasner, "Organized Hypocrisy in Nineteenth-Century East Asia," *International Relations of the Asia-Pacific* 1 (2001): 181.
26 Jones, *Extraterritoriality*, 2–3.
27 Ibid., 5–6.
28 Immanuel Hsü, *China's Entrance into the Family of Nations: The Diplomatic Phase, 1858–1880* (Cambridge, MA: Harvard University Press, 1959), 139.
29 Harris is known to have been biased against European countries, especially against Great Britain.
30 Following the United States, the Dutch signed a similar treaty on August 18, as did Russia on August 19, and France on October 9 in the same year.

31 The second chapter of Wheaton's *Elements of International Law* elaborates on the consular jurisdiction in the US-China Treaty of Amity and Commerce, clearly stating that as a general rule "civilised" states will never permit other countries' interference with their own legal rights, but that consular jurisdiction was applied to Turkey and Muslim countries in North Africa. Henry Wheaton, *Elements of International Law* (Boston: Little Brown and Company, 1866).

32 Motegi, *Henyō suru Kindai Higashi Ajia,* 32–43.

33 Gong, *The Standard of "Civilization,"* 164–200.

34 Martin's translation was based on the reprinted version published in 1857. Involved in drafting the commercial treaty between China and the United States 1858, Martin had strongly felt the need to provide the Chinese with knowledge of international law.

35 Japan may have had obtained the Chinese translation of Vattel's *International Law* translated by an American missionary, Peter Parker, in 1839 before Wheaton's translation.

36 Uriu Mitora's work in 1868 and Shigeno Yasutsugu's work in1870 are such examples.

37 Theodore Dwight Woolsey, *Introduction to the Study of International Law: Designed as an Aid in Teaching and in Historical Studies* (New York: C. Scribner, 1864); Charles de Marten, *Le guide diplomatique: précis des droits et des fonctions des agents diplomatiques* (Leipzig: F.A. Brockhaus, 1832).

38 Ryōichi Taoka, "Nishi Shūsuke 'Bankoku Kōhō'[Nishi Shūsuke's 'Law of Nations'']," *The Journal of Law and Diplomacy* 70, no.2 (1972).

39 This has been mentioned by many scholars who have examined Wheaton's original and Martin's translation. See, for example, Yoshihito Sumiyoshi, "Meiji Shokini okeru Kokusaihō no Dōnyū [Introduction of International Law in the Early Meiji]," *The Journal of Law and Diplomacy* 70, no.2 (1972).

40 Hsü, *China's Entrance,* 126. The quoted part is cited from M. E. Boggs, "William Alexander Parsons Martin, Missionary to China, 1850–1916," M.A. thesis (Chicago: Presbyterian College of Education, 1948), Appendix, 34.

41 Anonymous, "The Life and Work of the Late Dr. W.A.P. Martin," *The Chinese Recorder* 48, no. 1 (February 1917), cited in Hsü, *China's Entrance,* 138.

42 On learning about Martin's translation of Wheaton, the French chargé d'affaire, M. Klecskowsky, is said to have protested by saying, "Who is this man who is going to give the Chinese an insight into our European international law? Kill him – choke him off; he will make us endless trouble." William Alexander Parsons Martin, *A Cycle of Cathay: China, South and North, with Personal Reminiscences* (Whitefish: Kessinger Publishing, 1896), 234.

43 Shūsuke Nishi, *Professor Vissering's Lecture on International Law* (Tokyo: Kanhanshoseki Seihonsho, 1868). Nishi was not just a student of international law, but was also encyclopedic and versatile, contributing to many different fields such as aesthetics, philosophy, history, psychology, economics, and politics during the new era of Meiji government. Vissering was also a versatile scholar, who is said to have been influenced by Professor Heffter in the area of international law, the most authoritative figure in the field at that time.

44 Taoka, ["Nishi Shūsuke's"].

45 The term *"bankoku kōhō"* was the direct adoption from the Chinese translation, "Wang Guo Kang Fa."

46 Martin also translated Woolsey three years after Mitsukuri, making it easy to read and publishing the work in Japan in 1878. Sumiyoshi mentions that a big difference exists between Mitsukuri's and Martin's translations. Martin, for example, still used the word *"koho,"* or public law, reflecting the strong inclination of China to emphasise natural international law. Sumiyoshi, ["Introduction of International Law"], 454–79.

47 Takahashi Sakuye emphasises the infancy of Japan's understanding of international law at this time. He states that Japan was so weak in power and so inexperienced in the study of international law that it declared neutrality at the request of the French chargé d'affaire, relying on some parts of Martin's translation, without ever understanding what neutrality meant. Shigeru Kōzai, "Japan's Early Practice of International Law: The Law of Neutrality," *International Studies* (The International Studies Association of Ōsaka Gakuin University) 7, no. 1 (June 1996).

48 Sumiyoshi emphasises that it took a long time for Japan to understand European positivism due to the fact that Martin's translation first came to Japan and that Japanese social and ideological backgrounds tended to conform to naturalist law. Taoka, on the other hand, takes the position that the influence of naturalist thinking did not last long due to the introduction of positivism through Nishi and others. Sumiyoshi, ["Introduction of International Law"]; Taoka, ["Nishi Shūsuke's"].

49 The *Iroha-maru* incident occurred when the ship *Iroha-maru*, owned by the shipping company established by Sakamoto that became the first joint-stock corporation in Japan, *Kaien-tai*, collided with *Meiko-maru*, a ship owned by the Wakayama domain. After intense negotiations based on the facts written in logbooks, the Wakayama domain finally gave in and paid compensation. It is considered an incident that displayed Sakamoto's unusual political skills in maneuvering difficult negotiations. Sakamoto also tried to translate Wheaton's *Elements of International Law* and publish it by *Kaientai.*

50 Mary Elizabeth Berry, "Public Life in Authoritarian Japan," *Daedalus* 127 (Summer 1998): 133–65.

51 Quite a few books touch on the elements of the "functional equivalents" that Japan had possessed. See, for example, Berry, *Japan in Print*; Botzman, *Punishment and Power*; and Francks, *The Japanese Consumer*.

52 Related to this point, the closed nature of Japan (*sakoku*) before the arrival of Perry has been a major area of contention among scholars, as some point out the openness and curiosity of the Japanese towards the outside world even during the isolation period. For discussions on the nature of *sakoku* and on the status of Japan and Asia in the world, see, for example, Heita Kawakatsu, *Bunmei no Kaiyōshikan* [Maritime View of Civilisation] (Tokyo: Chūō Kōronsha, 1997); Takanori Irie, *Taiheiyo Bunmei no Kōbō* [Rise and Fall of the Pacific Civilisation] (Tokyo: PHP, 1997); Takashi Kobayashi, *Umi no Ajiashi* [Asian History from the Perspective of the Sea] (Tokyo: Fujiwara Shoten, 1997); Akira Hayami, Osamu Saitō, and Ronald P. Toby, *Emergence of Economic Society in Japan, 1600–1859* (Oxford: Oxford University Press, 2004); Bob T. Wakabayashi, *Anti-Foreignism and Western Learning in Early-Modern Japan: The New Theses of 1825* (Cambridge, MA: Harvard University Press, 1992); Ronald P. Toby, *State and Diplomacy in Early Modern Japan: Asia in the Development of the Tokugawa Bakufu* (Stanford, CA: Stanford University Press, 1984).

53 Marius B. Jansen, *Sakamoto Ryōma and the Meiji Restoration* (New York: Columbia University Press, 1995), 375–76.

54 Jansen, *The Making of Modern Japan*, 310.

55 The artificial fan-shaped land created for the Portugese merchants in 1636. The Dutch were moved there from Hirato in 1641 after Portugese ships were banned and became the only trading port in Japan during the isolation period.

56 Georg Friedrich Martens, *Primae lineae iuris gentium europaearum practici* [Summary of the Law of Nations Founded on the Treaties and Customs of the Modern Nations of Europe]. (Philadelphia: T. Bradford, 1795); Johann Jakob Moser, *Versuch des neuesten europaischen Volker-Rechts in Friedens- und Kriegs-Zeiten* [Experiment of the Newest European International Law in Peace -and War- Times] (Tode Kayser Carls, 1740).

Chapter 4

1 With Britain and Russia, the date was set on May 26, 1872, with the United States and the Netherlands on May 29, 1872, and with France on July 12, 1872.

2 Komon Tada, ed., *Iwakura Ko Jikki* [A True Record of Prince Iwakura] (Tokyo: Hara Shobo, 1968), vol. 2, 696–701.

3 Ian Nish, *Japanese Foreign Policy 1869–1942* (London: Routledge and Kegan Paul, 1977), 10.

4 Ibid., 20.

5 The negotiations that started on March 11, 1872, ended on July 22 of the same year. Kume Kunitake, *Beiō Kairan Jikki* [Commentary on America and Europe] (Tokyo: Iwanami Bunko, 2002), vol. 1. The English translation is also available. Kume Kunitake, *The Iwakura Embassy, 1871–73: A True Account of the Ambassador Extraordinary & Plenipotentiary's Journey of Observation through the United States of America and Europe,* trans. and ed. Graham Healey and Tsuzuki Chūshichi (Matsudo: The Japan Documents, 2002).

6 Ibid., vols. 1–5. Impressive in the accuracy and the detailed knowledge of various aspects of Western societies that the delegation observed, his records are excellent sources of study concerning Japan's enthusiasm about learning from the West and its devotion to modern nation building.

7 Kume, *Beiō Kairan Jikki* 3: 329–30. Here I have borrowed the translation that appears in Stern, *The Japanese Interpretation*, 88–89.

8 Shizuo Seki, ed., *Kindai Nihon Gaikō Shisōshi Nyūmon* [Introduction to the History of Modern Japanese Diplomatic Thought] (Tokyo: Minerva Publishing Company, 1999).

9 Nish states that "Iwakura returned not a cowed man but a confident one, aware that Japan had more effectively coped with the challenge of the West than China. If she had feelings of inferiority, her feeling of superiority to China was double confirmed" (*Japanese Foreign Policy,* 24).

10 Ibid., 21.

11 Okubo was one of the politicians who were strongly influenced by Bismarck's style of politics. He took an initiative in conducting various reforms to modernise Japan's political systems.

12 Jansen, *The Making of Modern Japan*, 59.

13 Dudden, "Japan's Engagement," 165.

14 The Ryūkyūan king, in fact, had a residence in Edo as did all the other daimyos during the Edo period.

15 Roy Hidemichi Akagi, *Japan's Foreign Relations 1542–1936: A Short History* (Tokyo: The Hokuseido Press, 1936) 69–70.

16 Akagi, *Japan's Foreign Relations*, 72. Western powers also protested the expedition due to their position of neutrality in Sino-Japanese affairs.

17 The foreign advisors employed by the government during the modernisation period were called "*oyatoi*," literally meaning "the employed." Ōkubo

is said to have treated him as a living reference book. Stern, *The Japanese Interpretation,* 120.

18 *Ōkubo Toshimichi Nikki* [A Diary of Ōkubo Toshimichi] (Tokyo: Hokusen-sha, 1997).

19 China's diplomatic authority and its equivalent of a foreign ministry.

20 Stern, *The Japanese Interpretation,* 122.

21 A Chinese currency unit. The value of one tael was 37.7 grams of silver.

22 Although Okubo's initial plan to send troops to Taiwan was canceled due to U.S. disapproval, Saigo Tsugumichi sent an expedition at his own discretion in 1874 and occupied Taiwan.

23 Stern, *The Japanese Interpretation,* 120.

24 Stern mentions how vigorously Ōkubo tried to appeal to the Western countries by developing friendly relations with them and controlling their opinions. Ōkubo "made fast friends with the French Minister on his arrival in Tientsin, and stayed at the American Ministry while in Beijing. The first day after his opening talks with the Zonli Yamen, Ōkubo made a good will tour of the Russian, American, and British legations; his diary records that Thomas Wade, and the Russian minister, and the Prussian minister soon came to him to discuss the talks." When the negotiations with China were about to end in hostilities, Ōkubo managed to bring in Wade to support Japan's diplomatic objectives. Ōkubo frankly admits that he "used" Wade. Ibid., 120–27.

25 Those who insisted on punishment included Saigō Tsugumichi and Itagaki Taisuke. They proposed the use of the military if Korea refused to open the country. Ōkubo and Kido, former members of the Iwakura Mission, opposed this on pragmatic grounds. According to Nish, "for the seventies, they felt that bearing in mind Japan's national weakness, she must abjure a policy of conquests in East Asia" (*Japanese Foreign Policy,* 24).

26 Jansen, *The Making of Modern Japan,* 424.

27 Stern, *The Japanese Interpretation,* 133–34.

28 Akagi, *Japan's Foreign Relations,* 65.

29 Nish notes that "Japan was not as much under foreign tutelage as he liked to emphasise; nor were the Western Powers as anxious to take over Japan as he feared. But the threat was grist to his mill: it enabled him to appeal to his countrymen to increase their wealth and strength on Western lines" (*Japanese Foreign Policy,* 12).

30 Numerous studies have been conducted on these foreign employees. See, for example, Noboru Umetani, *Oyatoi Gaikoku-jin* [Employed Foreigners] (Tokyo: Kashima-kenkyūjo Shuppankai, 1968); and *Oyatoi Gaikoku-jin: Meiji Nippon no Wakiyaku* [Employed Foreigners: Supporting Players of

Meiji Japan] (Tokyo: Nihon Keizai Shinbunsha, 1965); Ardath W. Burks, ed., *The Modernizers: Overeas Studients, Foreign Employees, and Meiji Japan* (Boulder, CO: Westview Press, 1985); Clark L. Beck and Ardath W. Burks, *Aspects of Meiji Modernization: The Japan Helpers and the Helped* (Piscataway, NJ: Transaction Publishers, 1983).

31 Gong, *The Standard of "Civilization,"* 187.

32 Foreign Minister Terajima Munenori signed the treaty after the negotiations between Yoshida Kiyonori (minister-counselor to the United States) and William Everts (secretary of state of the United States). The treaty, however, never came into effect.

33 Gong, *The Standard of "Civilization,"* 188.

Chapter 5

1 Yukichi Fukuzawa, *Bunmeiron no Gairyaku* [An Outline of Theories of Civilization] (Tokyo: Iwanami Bunko, 1995). *Datsuaron* [Theory of Leaving Asia] appeared as an editorial in *Jijishinpō* newspaper on March 16, 1885. Other advocates include Mori Arinori, who is said to have asked the great powers in 1879 to separate Japan's interests from those of Asia in general, and Tokutomi Sohō, who mentioned in the same year that Japan needed to take independent actions in order to avoid the fate of China.

2 Cholera was first brought after the Meiji Restoration by the US ship *Mississippi,* which came to Japan via China in 1877.

3 The best example that illustrates Inoue's obsession with the Westernisation of Japan is the famous *Rokumeikan* [Hall of the Baying Stag], which opened in July 1883. The dance parties held there were considered to be the epitome of the overt Westernisation of Inoue's style, often criticised as "flirtatious diplomacy."

4 Memorandum by Kanjō Tani (July 3, 1887), *Nihon Gaikō Monjo* 20, no. 26.

5 Inoue's response to Tani's memorandum, July 9, 1887, ibid.

6 Nish, *Japanese Foreign Policy,* 29. On the part of politicians "striving to influence the constitution in favour of popular rights," however, they wanted to delay the renegotiation of the treaties until the Diet was established.

7 In a letter that he wrote during his stay in the United States between 1870 and 1871, Itō says that Japan became fully equal with other civilised nations in the use of international law by the Meiji Restoration. This was the perception Itō held toward international law, the international system, and Japan's status in it. Shunpokō Tsuishōkai, *Itō Hitobumi Den* [Biography of Itō Hirobumi] (Tokyo: Tōseisha, 1940), 81. Letter of April 17, 1871. He

always emphasised the importance of using international legal logic in the discussions over treaty revision. Dudden, "Japan's Engagement," 178–80.

8 Nish, *Japanese Foreign Policy,* 31–32.

9 Ibid., 47.

10 From Aoki to Mutsu, *Nihon Gaikō Monjo* 27/I, no. 56 (July 19, 1894).

11 Another significant factor lingering behind that led to British consent to the reform was its anti-Russia policy. Afraid of Russia's increasing interest in East Asia, Britain needed to approach Japan in order to counter Russian expansion. Aoki's anti-Russian perception, in fact, blended well with the British suspicion toward Russia.

12 Nish, *Japanese Foreign Policy,* 29.

13 Ibid., 30.

14 Sano Tsunetami, who had established the *Hakuaisha* (literally, "Philanthropic Organisation"), made it into the Japan Red Cross.

15 Another interpretation of Japanese motives for the war is its colonial intentions and imperialism against Korea and China. Still other interpretation of the war is that Japan only needed to maintain Korea's neutrality for the purpose of its security and that China's insistence on its suzerainty was the cause of the problem. From a systemic viewpoint it could also be considered a hegemonic war in East Asia that replaced a worn-out order with a new rising order.

16 It had been decided by the treaty that, if there were a civil war in Korea and if China or Japan needed to send troops, they would exchange official letters to notify each other, and that when the turmoil died down, both would withdraw.

17 Nagao Ariga, *Bankoku Senji Kōhō* [International Laws of War] (Tokyo: National Academy of Army, 1894); Shingo Nakamura, *Kōwa Ruirei* [Cases of Peace Treaties] (Tokyo: Tetsugaku Shoin, 1895).

18 From Aoki to Mutsu, *Nihon Gaikō Monjo* (July 19, 1894).

19 Nagao Ariga, *La guerre sino-japonaise au point de vue du droit international* (Paris: A Pedone, 1896).

20 Ibid., ch. 1.

21 Hisakazu Fujita, "Nihon ni okeru Sensōhō Kenkyū no Ayumi [History of the Japanese War-time International Law]," *The Journal of International Law and Diplomacy* 96, nos. 4/5 (1997).

22 Sakuye Takahashi, *International Law during the Chino-Japanese War* (Cambridge: Cambridge University Press, 1899), 4.

23 His interpretation of the Russo-Japanese War was different from that of the Sino-Japanese War. He considered the former as a war between civilised states and named it a "civilised war," defining it as a war fought for the

purpose of the nation and national development with the instruments of civilised war, which occurred due to the mutual exclusiveness of the national interests of each country. Japan understood that, in such a war, unnecessary cruelty in treating war prisoners or other people should be prohibited and that it is a war between countries and not between peoples. Japan's interpretation of "civilised war" is basically an adoption of modern nineteenth-century European war.

24 Gong notes that Japanese efforts in conducting the 1894 Sino-Japanese War and the 1904 Russo-Japanese War according to the laws of war "won her the plaudits of Europe." Gong, *The Standard of "Civilization,"* 28.

25 T. E. Holland, *Studies in International Law* (Oxford: Clarendon Press, 1898), 112–14.

26 Takahashi, *International Law*, xvi; John Westlake, *Principles of International Law* (Cambridge: Cambridge University Press, 1894).

27 Henry Wheaton, *Elements of International Law,* 4th ed., ed. Beresford J. Atlay (London: Stevens & Sons, 1904).

28 Lassa Francis Oppenheim, "Non-Christian States," *International Law: A Treatise* 1 (London: Longmans, Green, and Co., 1912), ch. 9; Robert Phillimore, *Commentaries upon International Law* 3 (London: Butterworth, 1885).

29 Gong, *The Standard of "Civilization,"* 196–97.

30 Ibid., 197. Gong notes, for example, "When the great powers began claiming ports in China in the same territory that they had prevented Japan from occupying, e.g., Weihaiwei, Port Authur, and Kiaochow, their blatant hypocrisy rubbed salt into old Japanese wounds."

31 A letter written by a Westerner in *The Times* of December 28, 1889, for example, argued that "it is no exaggeration to say that the administration of justice, as understood by us, is wholly foreign to them, to their habits, their traditions, and their modes of thought." Gong, *The Standard of "Civilization,"* 188.

32 Speech by Ōkuma to the 11th Diet. Alfred Stead, ed., *Japan by Japanese: A Survey by Its Highest Authorities* (New York: Dodd, Mead, 1904), 219–21.

33 Sakuye Takahashi, *Senji Kokusaihōri Senreiron* [Cases on War-time International Legal Theory] (1904).

34 From Aoki to Mutsu, *Nihon Gaikō Monjo* (July 19, 1894).

35 These exchanges of letters and memoranda are available at the Foreign Policy Documentation Center in Japan.

36 On June 30, 1899. Ministerie van Buitenlandse Zaken: A-dossiers, 1815–1940, Bestanddeel: 520. Nationaal Archief, Den Haag, The Netherlands. I examined all the files 509–531 on the Hague Conference of 1899 in the Netherlands.

37 Bestanddeel: 529 shows the Japanese delegate Motono arguing for the protection of wounded soldiers on the basis of the 1864 Geneva Convention, which was taken up for discussion in the committee. Ariga Nagao accompanied the delegate as an expert on international law.

38 R. P. Anand, "Attitude of the Asian-African Countries toward Certain Problems of International Law," *International Comparative Law Quarterly* 15 (1966): 60.

39 While Japan received a small share of indemnities of the rebellion, its capability to suppress the uprising successfully in concert with the Western powers won it a reputation for qualified membership in international society. Akagi, *Japan's Foreign Relations*, 186–90.

40 Gong, *The Standard of "Civilization,"* 28.

Chapter 6

1 See, for example, Amino, *Nihon no Rekishi wo Yominaosu*.

2 See, for example, Fairbank, Reischauer, and Craig, *East Asia*, 185.

3 Yukichi Fukuzawa, *Fukuō Jiden* [Autobiography of Fukuzawa Yukichi] (Tokyo: Iwanami, 1978) 116–17 (translated by the author). He writes, for example, that the delegation was totally at a loss when they saw no American caring much about who the descendents of President Washington are. For more about Fukuzawa as a brilliant interpreter of Western culture and civilisation, see Craig, *Civilization and Enlightenment*. In a conversation with Craig, I learned that Fukuzawa's views actually changed over time from his early infatuation with Western culture to a more realistic understanding of it in his later life, when this autobiography was written.

4 Ibid., 110–22.

5 Fairbank, Reischauer, and Craig, *East Asia*, 189–91.

6 M. Bito, *Edo Jidai to wa Nanika* [What is the Edo Period?] (Tokyo: Iwanami, 1992).

7 A. Hayami and M. Miyamoto, *Nihon Keizai Shi* [Japanese Economic History] (Tokyo: Iwanami, 1988), vol. 1 ("Keizai Shakai no Seiritsu [The Establishment of Economic Society]").

8 Steinmo and Thelen, "Historical Institutionalism," 16–17.

9 For the social capital argument in general, see, for example, James Coleman, *Foundation of Social Theory* (Cambridge, MA: Belknap Press of Harvard University Press, 1990); Robert D. Putnam, *Making Democracy Work: Civic Traditions in Modern Italy* (Princeton, NJ: Princeton University Press, 1993); Francis Fukuyama, *Trust: The Social Virtues and Creation of Prosperity* (New York: Free Press, 1995).

10 See, for example, Berry, *Japan in Print*;and "Public Life in Authoritarian Japan," *Daedalus* 127 (Summer 1998): 133–65.

11 Coleman, *Foundation of Social Theory*; Putnam, *Making Democracy Work*; Fukuyama, *Trust*.

12 He uses the term "functional attributes" and characterises them as varying, "depending upon the nature of the environment that surrounds" them. "The defining characteristics ... must be identified at the core of the entity/concept and must transcend such contextual variations." They include a professional bureaucracy, a standing army, a monopoly of coercive resources, a unitary judicial system and powers of taxation. Masaru Kohno, "On the Meiji Restoration: Japan's Search for Sovereignty?" *International Relations of the Asia-Pacific* 1 (2001): 271.

13 The incident occurred on September 14, 1862, when one of the bodyguards of *daimyo* from the Satsuma domain slashed at British merchant Charles L. Richardson, who did not dismount his horse to show respect and got too close to the procession of the *daimyo*. The bodyguard's action was based on the traditional Japanese legal right to kill those who are disrespectful. The incident led to the Anglo-Satsuma War, as a result of which Satsuma domain paid compensation to Britain.

14 See Amitav Acharya's view on norm localisation: "How Ideas Spread: Whose Norms Matter? Norm Localization and Institutional Change in Asian Regionalism," *International Organization* 58 (Spring 2004): 241.

15 Nish, *Japanese Foreign Policy*, 25.

16 Major domestic turmoil included the rebellion led by Ōshio Heihachirō to save the poor in 1837. Peasants' uprisings had occurred in 1733, 1783, 1784, 1787, and 1836. Other revolts and riots due to inflation, crop failure, and famine occurred in 1652, 1712, 1723, 1754, 1764, 1781, 1793, and 1825.

17 Nish, *Japanese Foreign Policy*, 3–4.

18 Dudden, "Japan's Engagement," 178–80.

19 Akira Iriye, *China and Japan in the Global Setting* (Cambridge, MA: Harvard University Press, 1992), 30.

20 Since the end of the Edo period, many leaders had made great efforts to learn Western languages at schools called "juku," starting with Dutch and gradually shifting to English. Teki-juku of Professor Ogata Kōan in Ōsaka was one of the most famous "jukus" that produced many important figures during the early Meiji, including Fukuzawa Yukichi mentioned previously and Ōmura Masujirō (then Murata Zōroku).

21 Acharya, "How Ideas Spread."

22 Ibid.; Finnemore and Sikkink, "International Norm Dynamics," 897.

23 The importance of leaders' role in conformance with international norms has been noted by several scholars who are concerned with states' compliant behaviour. Previously mentioned, Ikenberry and Kupchan, for example, state that "elite receptivity" is essential to the socialisation process and for norms to have impact on state behaviour ("Socialization and Hegemonic Power," 284).
24 Fisch, "The Role of International Law," 5.
25 C. H. Alexandrowicz, *The European-African Confrontation* (Leiden: A.W. Sijthoff, 1973), 6.
26 W. E. Hall, *A Treatise on International Law*, 4th ed. (London: Stevens and Sons, 1895); Thomas Lawrence, *The Principles of International Law* (London: Macmillan, 1895); Lassa Oppenheim, *International Law* (London: Longmans, Green, 1905); John Westlake, *Principles of International Law* (Cambridge: Cambridge University Press, 1894).
27 Anghie, "Finding the Peripheries," 2.
28 Fisch, "The Role of International Law," 13.
29 Tilly, "Reflections on the History."
30 Anghie categorises several forms of socialisation with Western international society under positivist constraints: becoming a colony; concluding unequal treaties (under legal positivism, it was legal to use coercive means to compel other countries to conclude treaties that were mutually binding); meeting the standard of civilisation and joining the European club. Anghie, "Finding the Peripheries," 20–28.
31 For historical institutionalism, see, for example, Steinmo and Thelen, "Historical Institutionalism in Comparative Politics"; Peter Hall and Rosemary C. R. Taylor, "The Potential of Historical Institutionalism: A Response to Hay and Winscott," *Political Studies* 46, no. 5 (February, 2002): 958–62.
32 Finnemore and Sikkink, "International Norm Dynamics," 913.
33 Finnemore and Sikkink, therefore, argue that the processes of actors' choice in complying with norms involve a different kind of reasoning than that of utility maximization. Actors may ask themselves, "'What kind of situation is this?' and 'What am I supposed to do now?' Rather than 'How do I get what I want?' Actors often must choose between very different duties, obligations, rights, and responsibilities with huge social consequences, but understanding the choice depends on an understanding, not of utility maximization, but of social norms and rules that structure that choice." Ibid., 914.
34 A negative side of the story must also be noted. As Barrington Moore points out, Japan's militarism and the consequent policy failure inevitably occurred as a result of rapid, top-led nation building (Moore, *Social Origins*, ch. 4).

35 Jackson, *Quasi-states*; Mohammed Ayoob, *The Third World Security Predicament: State Making, Regional Conflict and the International System* (Boulder: Lynne Rienner, 1995).

36 Jackson, *Quasi-states*.

37 The *New York Times* (January 17, 1872). As many Japanese men started to cut off their topknots during the early Meiji, many wives divorced their husbands due to the shock inflicted by the new hairstyle. "*Danpatsu rikon* (divorce due to the cut topknot)" became a social phenomenon, causing a tremendous upheaval in Japan. After the Meiji emperor had his hair cut in 1873, the Western hairstyle spread nationwide.

38 Cameron G. Thies, "Sense and Sensibility in the Study of State Socialisation: A Reply to Kai Alderson," *Review of International Studies* 29 (2003): 547–48.

39 Anghie, "Finding the Peripheries," 36. Anghie emphasises the perpetuity of colonialism and interprets the creation of the nineteenth-century international law as centered around it. He suggests that "Colonial encounter, far from being peripheral to the making of international law, has been central to the formation of the discipline" (44).

40 Gong, *The Standard of "Civilization,"* 29.

41 Ibid., ch. 7.

42 Jackson calls them "positive sovereignty game" and "negative sovereignty game" (*Quasi-states*).

43 In order to see the institutional dynamics of international society more completely, further studies will be required on the side of the norm provider, the West. Few studies so far have treated the logic on the part of the socialisers.

44 Gong, *The Standard of "Civilization,"* 9.

Chapter 7

1 Spruyt, *The Sovereign State*.

2 Jackson and Rosberg, "Why Africa's Weak States Persist"; Jackson, *Quasi-states*.

3 Due to these changes in international structure and norms, the frequency of interstate wars was dramatically decreased, resulting in less common changes in international borders and lowered "death rates" of states. In particular, international borders have been stabilised with the incorporation of the right of self-determination in United Nations (UN) Charter and resolutions of the UN General Assembly, where the norms of inviolability of state borders were explicitly stated and institutionalised.

4 Jackson and Rosberg, "Why Africa's Weak States Persist"; Jackson, *Quasi-states.*

5 Ayoob, *The Third World Security Predicament.*

6 Tilly, "War-making and State-making."

7 For problems on case studies, see George and Bennett, *Case Studies;* Gary King, Robert O. Keohane, and Sidney Verba, *Designing Social Inquiry: Scientific Inference in Qualitative Research* (Princeton, NJ: Princeton University Press, 1994). George and Bennett offer more sympathetic views on single-case studies.

8 Johnston, "Treating International Institutions."

9 Theophile Delcasse is known as an anti-German diplomat who tried to strengthen French ties with Russia. This proposal was largely due to the fact that France was the biggest creditor power for Russia. Worried about the prospect of war, France unilaterally declared the no-time-limit postponement of undertaking Russian bonds after they heard of Japan's victory in the battle of Fengtien. France feared that, if Japan demanded compensation, Russia would use the money it borrowed from France for the compensation and that France would never get even the warranty of the capital. For further studies on Delcasse's diplomacy, see, for example, C. Andrew, *Theophile Delcasse and the Making of the Entente Cordiale: Reappraisal of French Foreign Policy, 1898–1925* (London: Macmillan, 1968); Graham H. Stuart, *French Foreign Policy for Fashoda to Serajevo, 1898–1914* (Charleston: Biblio Bazaar, 2009).

10 Today's Liaoning Province in China.

11 Japan itself had records of paying due compensations to the West. When Chōshū domain fought against the four powers and when Satsuma domain fought against the Britain, the *bakufu* paid the fee. Even after the *bakufu* was overthrown, the newly established Meiji government paid the unpaid part of the compensation.

12 Gong, *The Standard of "Civilization,"* 165.

13 For the Japanese foreign policy behaviour of the 1930s, see, for example, F. C. Jones, *Japan's New Order in East Asia: Its Rise and Fall, 1937–1945* (London: Oxford University Press, 1954); Richard Storry, *The Double Patriots* (London: Chatto and Windus, 1957); Herbert Feis, *The Road to Pearl Harbor* (Princeton, NJ: Princeton University Press, 1950).

14 Ichirō Ozawa, "Futsūno no Kuni ni Nare [Become a Normal Country]," *Sengo Nihon Gaikō Ronshu [Postwar Japanese Diplomatic Writings],* ed. Shin'ichi Kitaoka (Tokyo: Chūō Kōron Sha, 1995).

15 Fisch, "The Role of International Law," 5.

16 Stephen D. Krasner, "Economic Interdependence and Independent Statehood," in *States in a Changing World: A Contemporary Analysis*, ed. Robert H. Jackson and Alan James (Oxford: Clarendon, 1993), 318.

17 Krasner, *Sovereignty*.

Selected Bibliography

Sources in English

Abi-Saab, Georges. "International Law and the International Community: The Long Road to Universality." In *Essays in Honor of Wang Tieya* 31. Edited by Ronald St. John Macdonald. Boston: M. Nijhoff, 1994.

Acharya, Amitav. "How Ideas Spread: Whose Norms Matter? Norm Localization and Institutional Change in Asian Regionalism." *International Organization* 58, no. 2 (2004): 239–275.

Akagi, Roy Hidemichi. *Japan's Foreign Relations 1542–1936*. Tokyo: Hokuseido Press, 1936.

Alderson, Kai. "Making Sense of State Socialisation." *Review of International Studies* 27, no. 3 (2001): 415–33.

Alexandrowicz, C. H. "Mogul Sovereignty and the Law of Nations." *Indian Yearbook of International Affairs* 4 (1955): 316–24.

Alexandrowicz, C. H. "Treaty and Diplomatic Relations between European and South Asian Powers in the Seventeenth and Eighteenth Centuries." *Recueil des Cours* 2 (1960): 207–8.

Alexandrowicz, C. H. "Some Problems of the History of the Law of Nations." *Indian Yearbook of International Relations* 12 (1963): 3–11.

Alexandrowicz, C. H. *An Introduction to the History of the Law of Nations in the East Indies*. Oxford: Oxford University Press, 1967.

Alexandrowicz, C. H. *The European-African Confrontation*. Leiden: A.W. Sijthoff, 1973.

Almond, Gabriel, and James Coleman, eds. *The Politics of Developing Areas*. Princeton, NJ: Princeton University Press, 1960.

Anand, R. P. "Universality of International Law: An Asian Perspective" in *Universality and Continuity in International Law*. Thilo Marauhn and Heinhard Steiger, eds. The Hague: Eleven International Publishing, 2011: 87–105.

Anand, R. P. "Attitude of the Asian-African Countries toward Certain Problems of International Law." *International and Comparative Law Quarterly* 15, no. 1 (1966): 55–75.

Anderson, Benedict. *The Spectre of Comparisons: Nationalism, Southeast Asia and the World*. London: Verso, 1998.

Anghie, Anthony. "Finding the Peripheries: Sovereignty and Colonialism in Nineteenth-Century International Law." *Harvard International Law Journal* 40 (Winter 1999): 1–80.

Anghie, Anthony. *Imperialism, Sovereignty and the Making of International Law*. Cambridge Studies in International and Comparative Law. Cambridge: Cambridge University Press, 2005.

Ariga, Nagao. *La guerre sino-japonaise au point de vue du droit international*. Paris: A. Pedone, 1896.

Auslin, Michael R. *Negotiating with Imperialism: The Unequal Treaties and the Culture of Japanese Diplomacy*. Cambridge, MA: Harvard University Press, 2004.

Ayoob, Mohammed. *The Third World Security Predicament: State Making, Regional Conflict and the International System*. Boulder, CO: Lynne Rienner, 1995.

Badie, Bertrand. *The Imported State: the Westernization of the Political Order*. Translated by Claudia Royal. Stanford, CA: Stanford University Press, 2000.

Baelz, Erwin, Toku Baelz, E. Paul, and C. Paul. *Awakening Japan: The Diary of a German Doctor*. Bloomington: Indiana University Press, 1974.

Banno, Masataka. *China and the West 1858–1861: The Origins of the Tsungli Yamen*. Cambridge, MA: Harvard University Press, 1964.

Bartlett, Thomas. *The Making of Europe: Conquest, Colonization, and Cultural Change*. Princeton, NJ: Princeton University Press, 1993.

Beasley, W. G. *Select Documents on Japanese Foreign Policy 1853–68*. London: Oxford University Press, 1967.

Beasley, W. G. *The Meiji Restoration*. Stanford, CA: Stanford University Press, 1973.

Beasley, W. G. *The Rise of Modern Japan*. London: Weidenfeld and Nicolson, 1990.

Bellah, Robert. *Tokugawa Religion: The Cultural Roots of Modern Japan*. New York: Free Press, 1985.

Benedict, Ruth. *The Chrysanthemum and the Sword*. Boston: Houghton Mifflin, 1946.

Bentham, Jeremy. *An Introduction to the Principles of International Law and Legislation*. Oxford: Clarendon Press, 1843.

Berger, P. L., and T. Luckmann. *The Social Construction of Reality: A Treatise in the Sociology of Knowledge*. New York: Anchor Books, 1966.

Berry, Mary Elizabeth. "Public Life in Authoritarian Japan." *Daedalus* 127 (Summer 1998): 133–65.

Berry, Mary Elizabeth. *Japan in Print: Information and Nation in the Early Modern Period*. Berkeley: University of California Press, 2006.

Botzman, Daniel V. *Punishment and Power in the Making of Modern Japan*. Princeton, NJ: Princeton University Press, 2005.

Brenner, T. "Can Evolutionary Algorithms Describe Learning Processes?" *Journal of Evolutionary Economics* 8, no. 3 (1998): 271–83.

Brown, Chris. "International Political Theory and the Idea of World Community." In *International Relations Theory Today*. Edited by Ken Booth and Steve Smith, 90–109. University Park: Pennsylvania State University Press, 1995.

Buckle, Henry Thomas. *History of Civilization in England*. 2 vols. New York: D. Appleton and Company, 1857–61.

Bull, Hedley. *Anarchical Society: A Study of Order in World Politics*. London: McMillan, 1977.

Bull, Hedley, and Adam Watson. *The Expansion of International Society*. Oxford: Oxford University Press, 1984.

Butterfield, Herbert, and Martin Wight, eds. *Diplomatic Investigations: Essays in the Theory of International Politics*. London: George Allen & Unwin, 1966.

Buzan, Barry, and Richard Little. "The Idea of 'International System': Theory Meets History." *International Political Science Review* 15, no. 3 (1994): 231–55.

Buzan, Barry, and Richard Little. *International Systems in World History: Remaking the Study of International Relations*. New York: Oxford University Press, 2000.

Buzan, Barry, Charles Jones, and Richard Little. *The Logic of Anarchy: Neorealism to Structural Realism*. New York: Columbia University Press, 1993.

Caporaso, J., ed. *The Elusive State*. Beverly Hills, CA: Sage Publications, 1989.

Carr, Edward H. *The Twenty Years' Crisis, 1919–1939: An Introduction to the Study of International Relations*. New York: Harper & Row, 1964.

Carty, Anthony. *The Decay of International Law?: A Reappraisal of the Limits of Legal Imagination in International Affairs*. Manchester: Manchester University Press, 1986.

Chang, R. T. *The Justice of the Western Consular Courts in Nineteenth-Century Japan*. Westport, CT: Greenwood Press, 1984.

Chan-Tiberghien, Jennifer. *Gender and Human Rights Politics in Japan: Global Norms and Domestic Networks*. Stanford, CA: Stanford University Press, 2004.

Chayes, Abram, and Antonia Handler Chayes. "On Compliance." *International Organization* 47, no. 2 (Spring 1993): 175–206.

Chinese Foreign Office. *Treaties, Conventions and Protocols between China and Foreign States*. Shanghai, 1917.

Chinkin, Christine M. "The Challenge of Soft-Law: Development and Change in International Law." *International and Comparative Law Quarterly* 38, no. 8 (1989): 50–66.

Coleman, James. *Foundation of Social Theory*. Cambridge, MA: Belknap Press of Harvard University Press, 1990.

Cortell, Andrew, and James W. Davis. "When Norms Clash: International Norms, Domestic Practices, and Japan's Internationalisation of the GATT/WTO." *Review of International Studies* 31, no. 1 (2005): 3–25.

Craig, Albert M. *Civilization and Enlightenment: The Early Thought of Fukuzawa Yukichi*. Cambridge, MA: Harvard University Press, 2009.

Craig, Albert M., and Donald H. Shively, eds. *Personality in Modern Japan*. Berkeley: University of California Press, 1979.

Craig, Gordon A. "The Historian and the Study of International Relations." *American Historical Review* 88, no. 1 (1983): 1–11.

Crasset, Jean. *Histoire de l'eglise du Japon*. Paris: Chez Estienne Michallet, 1689.

Crawford, James. *The Creation of States in International Law*. Oxford: Clarendon Press, 1979.

Dickinson, Edwin DeWitt. *The Equality of States in International Law*. Cambridge, MA: Harvard University Press, 1920.

Dower, John, ed. *Origins of the Modern Japanese State*. New York: Pantheon Books, 1975.

Dudden, Alexis. "Japan's Engagement with International Terms." In *Tokens of Exchange: The Problem of Translation in Global Circulations*. Edited by Lydia H. Liu. Durham, NC: Duke University Press, 1999.

Dunne, Tim. *Inventing International Society: A History of the English School*. Oxford: Macmillan, 1998.

Edwards, Michael. *Asia in the European Age 1498–1955*. London: Thames and Hudson, 1961.

Elman, Colin, and Mirium Fendius Elman, "Diplomatic History and International Relations Theory: Respecting Differences and Crossing Boundaries," *International Security* 22, no.1 (Summer, 1997).

Elman, Colin, and Mirium Fendius Elman, eds. *Bridges and Boundaries: Historians, Political Scientists, and the Study of International Relations*. Cambridge, MA: MIT Press, 2001.

Ertman, Thomas. *Birth of the Leviathan: Building States and Regimes in Medieval and Early Modern Europe*. Cambridge: Cambridge University Press, 1997.

Eskildsen, Robert. "Of Civilization and Savages: The Mimetic Imperialism of Japan's 1874 Expedition to Taiwan." *American Historical Review* 107, no. 2 (2002): 388–418.

Evans, Peter B., Harold K. Jacobson, and Robert D. Putnam, eds. *Double-Edged Diplomacy: International Bargaining and Domestic Politics.* Berkeley: University of California Press, 1993.

Fairbank, J. K., E. O. Reischauer, and A. M. Craig. *East Asia: The Modern Transformation*. Boston: Houghton Mifflin, 1965.

Fairbank, J. K. "Synarchy under the Treaties." In *Chinese Thought and Institutions*. Edited by J. K. Fairbank, 204–34. Chicago: University of Chicago Press, 1957.

Fairbank, J. K., ed. *The Chinese World Order*. Cambridge, MA: Harvard University Press, 1968.

Fauchille, Paul. *Traité de droit international public*. Paris: Lib. Authur Rousseau, 1925.

Feifer, George. *Breaking Open Japan: Commodore Perry, Lord Abe, and American Imperialism in 1853*. New York: Collins, 2006.

Feis, Herbert. *The Road to Pearl Harbor*. Princeton, NJ: Princeton University Press, 1950.

Finnemore, Martha, and Kathryn Sikkink. "International Norm Dynamics and Political Change." *International Organization* 52, no. 4 (1998): 887–917.

Finnemore, Martha. "Norms, Culture, and World Politics: Insights from Sociology's Institutionalism." *International Organization* 50, no. 2 (1996): 325.

Finnemore, Martha. *National Interest in International Society*. Ithaca, NY: Cornell University Press, 1996.

Fisch, Jörg. "The Role of International Law in the Territorial Expansion of Europe, 16th–20th Centuries." *ICCLP Review* 3, no. 1 (2000): 5–15.

Fishel, Wesley R. *The End of Extraterritoriality in China*. Berkeley: University of California Press, 1952.

Fitzgerald, Charles P. *The Chinese View of Their Place in the World*. London: Royal Institute of International Affairs, 1964.

Flowers, Petrice R. *Refugees, Women and Weapons:International Norm Adoption and Compliance in Japan*. Stanford, CA: Stanford University Press, 2009.

Francks, Penelope. *The Japanese Consumer: An Alternative Economic History of Modern Japan*. Cambridge: Cambridge University Press, 2009.

Freedman, P. E., and A. Freedman. "Political Learning." In *The Handbook of Political Behaviour 1*. Edited by S. Long. New York: Plenum Press, 1981.

Fukuyama, Francis. *Trust: The Social Virtues and Creation of Prosperity*. New York: Free Press, 1995.

Garner, James W. *Recent Developments in International Law: Tagore Law Lectures*. Calcutta: University of Calcutta Press, 1922.

Garon, Sheldon. "Rethinking Modernization and Modernity in Japanese History: A Focus on State-Society Relations." *Journal of Asian Studies* 53, no. 2 (May 1994): 346–66.

Gelber, Harry G. *The Dragon and the Foreign Devils in China and the World, 1100 B.C. to the Present*. New York: Walker & Company, 2007.

George, Alexander L., and Andrew Bennett. *Case Studies and Theory Development in the Social Sciences*. Cambridge, MA: MIT Press, 2005.

Gerschenkron, Alexander. *Economic Backwardness in Historical Perspective*. Cambridge, MA: Harvard University Press, 1962.

Gilbert, Rodney. *The Unequal Treaties*. London: John Murray, 1929.

Gluck, Carol. *Japan's Modern Myths:Ideology in the Late Meiji Period*. Princeton, NJ: Princeton University Press, 1985.

Goldsmith, J. L., and E. A. Posner. "A Theory of Customary International Law." *University of Chicago Law Review. University of Chicago. Law School* 66, no. 4 (1999): 1113–77.

Goldstein, Judith. L., Miles Kahler, Robert O. Keohane, and Anne-Marie Slaughter. *Legalization and World Politics*. Cambridge, MA: MIT Press, 2001.

Goldstein, Judith L., and Robert O. Keohane, eds. 1990. *Ideas and Foreign Policy: Beliefs, Institutions, and Political Change*. Ithaca, NY: Cornell University Press.

Gong, Gerrit. *The Standard of "Civilization" in International Society*. Oxford: Clarendon Press, 1984.

Gong, Gerrit. "Empires and Civilization." *International Studies Quarterly* 121 (2010): 144–46.

Goody, Jack. *The East in the West*. Cambridge: Cambridge University Press, 1996.

Gordon, Andrew. *A Modern History of Japan: From Tokugawa Times to the Present*. New York: Oxford University Press, 2009.

Gourevitch, Peter. "The Second Image Reversed: The International Sources of Domestic Politics." *International Organization* 32, no. 4 (1978): 881.

Grovogui, Siba N'Zatioula. *Sovereigns, Quasi Sovereigns, and Africans: Race and Self-Determination in International Law*. Minneapolis: University of Minnesota Press, 1996.

Guizot, François. *Histoire de la Civilisation en Europe* [General History of Civilisation in Europe]. Translated by C. S. Henry. New York: D.Appleton and Company, 1828.

Haggard, Stephen, and Beth Simmons. "Theories of International Regimes." *International Organization* 41, no. 3 (1987): 491–517.

Hall, John W. *Japanese History, New Dimensions of Approach and Understanding*. Washington, D.C.: Service Center for Teachers of History, 1961.

Hall, John W., and Marius Jansen. *Studies in the Institutional History of Early Modern Japan*. Princeton, NJ: Princeton University Press, 1970.

Hall, Peter A., and Rosemary C. R. Taylor. "Political Science and the Three New Institutionalisms." *Political Studies* 44, no. 5 (1996): 936–57.

Hall, Peter A., and Rosemary C. R. Taylor. "The Potential of Historical Institutionalism: A Response to Hay and Winscott." *Political Studies* 46, no. 5 (2002): 952–62.

Hall, W. E. *A Treatise on International Law*. 4th ed. London: Stevens and Sons, 1895.

Halliday, Jon. *A Political History of Japanese Capitalism*. New York: Pantheon, 1975.

Hardie, Frank. *The Abyssinian Crisis*. London: Batsford, 1974.

Hart, H.L.A. *Concept of Law*. Oxford: Clarendon Press, 1961.

Hayami, Akira, Osamu Saito, and Ronal P. Toby. *Emergence of Economic Society in Japan, 1600–1859*. Oxford: Oxford University Press, 2004.

Held, David, and Anthony McGrew. "The End of the Old Order? Globalization and the Prospects for World Order." In *The Eighty Years' Crisis: International Relations 1919–1999*. Edited by Tim Dunne, Michael Cox, and Ken Booth. Cambridge: Cambridge University Press, 1998.

Hill, Christopher. "History and International Relations." In *International Relations: British and American Perspectives*. Edited by Steve Smith. Oxford: Basil Blackwell, 1985.

Hill, Christopher. *National History and the World of Nations: Capital, State, and the Rhetoric of History in Japan, France, and the United States*. Durham, NC: Durham University Press, 2008.

Hillgenberg, Y. H. "A Fresh Look at Soft Law." *European Journal of International Law* 10, no. 3 (1999): 499–515.

Hirschman, Albert. *A Bias for Hope*. New Haven, CT: Yale University Press, 1971.

Hirschmeier, Johannes. *The Origins of Entrepreneurship in Meiji Japan*. Cambridge, MA: Harvard University Press, 1964.

Hirst, Paul, and G. Thompson. *Globalization in Question*. Cambridge: Cambridge University Press, 1996.

Hoare, James E. *Japan's Treaty Ports and Foreign Settlements: The Uninvited Guests, 1858–1899*. Kent: Japan Library, 1994.

Holland, T. E. *Studies in International Law*. Oxford: Clarendon Press, 1898.

Holland, T. E. *Lectures on International Law*. London: Sweet and Maxwell, 1933.

Holsti, K. J. "Scholarship in an Era of Anxiety: The Study of International Politics During the Cold War." In *The Eighty Years' Crisis: International Relations 1919–1999*. Edited by Tim Dunne, Michael Cox, and Ken Booth, 17–46. Cambridge: Cambridge University Press, 1998.

Holsti, K. J. *Taming the Sovereigns: Institutional Change in International Politics*. Cambridge: Cambridge University Press, 2004.

von Holzendorff, Franz. *Introduction au droit des gens: recherches philosophiques, historiques, et bibliographiques*. Hamburg: Verlag Somstaff und Druckerei, 1889.

Howard, Michael. *War in European History*. Oxford: Oxford University Press, 1976.

Howell, David Luke. *Capitalization from Within: Economy, Society, and the State in a Japanese Fishery*. Berkeley: University of California Press, 1995.

Howland, Douglas R. *Borders of Chinese Civilization: Geography and History at Empire's End*. Durham, NC: Duke University Press, 1996.

Howland, Douglas R. *Translating the West: Language and Political Reason in 19th-century Japan*. Honolulu: University of Hawaii Press, 2002.

Hsiung, James C. *Anarchy and Order: The Interplay of Politics and Law in International Relations*. Boulder, CO: Lynne Rienner, 1997.

Hsü, Immanuel. *China's Entrance into the Family of Nations: The Diplomatic Phase, 1860–1880*. Cambridge, MA: Harvard University Press, 1960.

Hudson, Manley O., ed. *International Legislation: A Collection of the Texts of Multipartite International Instruments of General Interest Beginning with the Covenant of the League of Nations*. Washington, D.C.: Carnegie Endowment for International Peace, 1931.

Hull, William I. *The Two Hague Conferences*. Boston: Ginn and Company, 1908.

Huntington, Samuel P. *Political Order in Changing Societies*. New Haven, CT: Yale University Press, 1968.

Hurrell, Andrew. "Conclusion: International Law and the Changing Constitution of International Society." In *The Role of Law in International Politics: Essays in International Relations and International Law*. Edited by Michael Byers, 327–46. Oxford: Oxford University Press, 2000.

Ichilov, O., ed. *Political Socialization, Citizenship Education and Democracy*. New York: Teachers College Press, 1990.

Ikenberry, G. John, and Charles A. Kupchan. "Socialization and Hegemonic Power." *International Organization* 44, no. 3 (1990): 283–315.

Iriye, Akira. *China and Japan in the Global Setting*. Cambridge, MA: Harvard University Press, 1992.

Irokawa, Daikichi. *The Culture of the Meiji Period*. Translated by M. B. Jansen. Princeton, NJ: Princeton University Press, 1985.

Jackson, Robert H., and Alan James, eds. *States in a Changing World: A Contemporary Analysis*. Oxford: Clarendon Press, 1993.

Jackson, Robert, and Carl Rosberg. "Sovereignty and Underdevelopment: Juridical Statehood in the African Crisis." *Journal of Modern African Studies* 24, no. 1 (1986): 1–31.

Jackson, Robert, and Carl G. Rosberg. "Why Africa's Weak States Persist: The Empirical and Juridical in Statehood." *World Politics* 35, no. 1 (1982): 1–24.

Jackson, Robert. *Quasi-states: Sovereignty, International Relations and the Third World*. Cambridge: Cambridge University Press, 1990.

Jacobson, Harold K. "International Institutions and System Transformation." *Annual Review of Political Science* 3, no. 1 (2000): 149–66.

Jansen, Marius B. *Changing Japanese Attitudes Toward Modernization*. Princeton, NJ: Princeton University Press, 1965.

Jansen, Marius B. *Sakamoto Ryoma and the Meiji Restoration*. New York: Columbia University Press, 1995.

Jansen, Marius B. *The Making of Modern Japan*. Cambridge, MA: Harvard University Press, 2002.

Job, Brian L., ed. *The Insecurity Dilemma: National Security of Third World States*. Boulder: Lynne Rienner Publishers, 1992.

Johnston, Alastair Iain. "Treating International Institutions as Social Environments." *International Studies Quarterly* 45, no. 4 (2001): 487–515.

Johnston, Alastair Iain. *Social States: China in International Institutions, 1980–2000*. Princeton, NJ: Princeton University Press, 2008.

Jones, Francis Clifford. *Japan's New Order in East Asia: Its Rise and Fall, 1937–1945*. London: Oxford University Press, 1954.

Jones, Francis Clifford. *Extraterritoriality in Japan and the Diplomatic Relations Resulting in Its Abolition 1853–1899*. New Haven, CT: AMS Press, 1970.

Katzenstein, Peter J. *Small States in World Markets: Industrial Policy in Europe*. Ithaca, NY: Cornell University Press, 1985.

Kayaoğlu, Turan. "International Norms, Territorial Sovereignty, and the Abolition of Extraterritoriality." Paper prepared for delivery at the Annual Meeting of the American Political Science Association, San Francisco, August 30–September 2, 2001.

Kayaoğlu, Turan. *Legal Imperialism: Sovereignty and Extraterritoriality in Japan, the Ottoman Empire, and China*. New York: Cambridge University Press, 2010.

Keeton, W. *The Development of Extraterritoriality in China*. New York: Howard Fertig, 1969.

Kennedy, David. *International Legal Structures*. Baden-Baden: Nomos Verlagsgesellschaft, 1987.

Keohane, Robert. *After Hegemony: Cooperation and Discord in the World Political Economy*. Princeton, NJ: Princeton University Press, 1986.

Keohane, Robert. "International Institutions: Two Approaches." *International Studies Quarterly* 32, no. 4 (1988): 379–96.

Keohane, Robert. "Neoliberal Institutionalism: A Perspective on World Politics." In *International Institutions and State Power: Essays in International Relations Theory*. Edited by Robert O. Keohane, 1–20. Boulder, CO: Westview Press, 1989.

Ker, W. "Treaty-Revision in Japan: A Survey of the Steps by Which the Abolition of Foreign Privilege was Accomplished in the Island Empire." *Pacific Affairs* 1, no. 6 (1928): 1–10.

Kim, Key-Hiuk. *The Last Phase of the East Asian World Order: Korea, Japan, and the Chinese Empire, 1860–1882*. Berkeley: University of California Press, 1980.

King, Gary, Robert O. Keohane, and Sidney Verba. *Designing Social Inquiry: Scientific Inference in Qualitative Research*. Princeton, NJ: Princeton University Press, 1994.

Koh, Harold, "Why Do Nations Obey International Law?" *Yale Law Journal* 106, no. 8 (1997): 2599–659.

Kohno, Masaru. "On the Meiji Restoration: Japan's Search for Sovereignty?" *International Relations of the Asia-Pacific* 1, no. 2 (2001): 265–83.

Koremenos, Barbara, Charles Lipson, and Duncan Snidal. "The Rational Design of International Institutions." *International Organization* 55, no. 4 (2001): 761–99.

Krasner, Stephen D. "Sovereignty: An Institutional Perspective." *Comparative Political Studies* 21, no. 1 (1988): 66–94.

Krasner, Stephen D. *Sovereignty: Organized Hypocrisy*. Princeton, NJ: Princeton University Press, 1999.

Krasner, Stephen D. "Organized Hypocrisy: Nineteenth-Century East Asia." *International Relations of the Asia-Pacific* 1, no. 2 (2001): 173–97.

Krasner, Stephen D. *Problematic Sovereignty: Contested Rules and Political Possibilities*. New York: Columbia University Press, 2001.

Kratochwil, Friedrich V. *Rules, Norms, and Decisions: On the Conditions of Practical and Legal Reasoning in International and Domestic Affairs*. Cambridge: Cambridge University Press, 1989.

Kume, Kunitake. *The Iwakura Embassy, 1871–73: A True Account of the Ambassador Extraordinary and Plenipotentiary's Journey of Observation through the United States of America and Europe*. Translated and edited by Graham Healey and Tsuzuki Chushichi. Matsudo: The Japan Documents, 2002.

Kunz, Josef L. "Pluralism of Legal and Value Systems and International Law." *American Journal of International Law* 49, no. 3 (1955): 370.

Lach, Donald F. *Japan in the Eyes of Europe: The Sixteenth Century*. Chicago: University of Chicago Press, 1968.

Lach, Donald F. *Asia in the Making of Europe*. Chicago: University of Chicago Press, 1965–93.

Langer, William L. *An Encyclopedia of World History: Ancient, Medieval, and Modern*. London: Harrap, 1972.

Lauterpacht, H. *Recognition in International Law*. Cambridge: Cambridge University Press, 1947.

Lawrence, Thomas. *The Principles of International Law*. London: Macmillan, 1895.

Lee, Kwang-rin. "The Introduction of the '*Wan-kuo kung-fa' to Korea*'." East Asian Studies] (The Journal of the Institute for East Asian Studies, Sogan University) (December, 1982): 121–45.

Leheny, David. *The Rules of Play: National Identity and the Shaping of Japanese Leisure*. Ithaca, NY: Cornell University Press, 2003.

Leifer, Michael, ed. *Asian Nationalism*. New York: Routledge, 2000.

Levi-Strauss, Claude. *Tristes Tropiques*. Translated by John Weightman and Doreen Weightman. New York: Penguin Books, 1992.

Levi-Strauss, Claude. *Structural Anthropology*. New York: Basic Books, 1963.

Lewis, Bernard. *The Emergence of Modern Turkey*. Oxford: Oxford University Press, 1962.

Lindley, M. F. *The Acquisition and Government of Backward Territory in International Law*. London: Longmans, Green, 1926.

Liu, Lydia H. *Translingual Practice: Literature, National Culture, and Translated Modernity—China 1900–1937*. Stanford, CA: Stanford University Press, 1995.

Liu, Lydia H. "Legislating the Universal: The Circulation of International Law in the Nineteenth Century." In *Tokens of Exchange: The Problem of Translation in Global Circulations*. Edited by Lydia Liu, 127–64. Durham, NC: Duke University Press, 1999.

Liu, Lydia H. "Desire for the Sovereign and the Logic of Reciprocity in the Family of Nations." *Diacritics* 29, no. 4 (1999): 150 77.

Liu, Shih-shun. *Extraterritoriality: Its Rise and Decline*. New York: Columbia University Press, 1925.

Lockwood, William. *The Economic Development of Japan: Growth and Structural Change, 1868–1938*. Princeton, NJ: Princeton University Press, 1954.

Lorimer, James. *Institutes of the Law of Nations*. Edinburgh: Blackwood and Sons, 1883.

Lowe, Vaughan. "The Politics of Law-Making: Are the Method and Character of Norm Creation Changing?" In *The Role of Law in International Politics: Essays in International Relations and International Law*. Edited by Michael Byers, 207–46. Oxford: Oxford University Press, 2000.

Luard, Evan. *Types of International Society*. New York: The Free Press, 1976.

Lyon, G. M., and Michael Mastanduno. *Beyond Westphalia: State Sovereignty and International Intervention*. New York: Johns Hopkins University Press, 1995.

March, James, and Johan P. Olsen. "The New Institutionalism: Organizational Factors in Political Life." *American Political Science Review* 78, no. 3 (1984): 734–49.

March, James, and Johan P. Olsen. *Rediscovering Institutions*. New York: Free Press, 1989.

Mayers, W. F., N. B. Dennys, and C. King. *The Treaty Ports of China and Japan*. London: Trubner, 1867.

McOmie, William. *The Opening of Japan, 1853–1855: A Comparative Study of the American, British, Dutch, and Russian Naval Expeditions to Compel the Tokugawa Shogunate to Conclude Treaties and Open Ports to their Ships*. Kent: Global Oriental, 2006.

Meyer, John W., John Boli, George M. Thomas, and Francisco Ramirez. "World Society and the Nation-State." *American Journal of Sociology* 103, no. 1 (1997): 144–81.

Milner, Helen V. *Interests, Institutions, and Information: Domestic Politics and International Relations*. Princeton, NJ: Princeton University Press, 1997.

Moore, Barrington. *Social Origins of Dictatorship and Democracy: Lord and Peasant in the Making of the Modern World*. Boston: Beacon Press, 1966.

Nardin, Terry. "International Pluralism and the Rule of Law." *Review of International Studies* 26, no. 5 (2000): 95–110.

Nish, Ian. *Japanese Foreign Policy 1869–1942*. London: Routledge and Kegan Paul, 1977.

North, Douglass C., and Robert Paul Thomas. *The Rise of the Western World: A New Economic History*. Cambridge: Cambridge University Press, 1973.

North, Douglass C. *Structure and Change in Economic History*. New York: Norton & Company, 1981.

North, Douglass C. *Institutions, Institutional Change and Economic Performance*. Cambridege: Cambridge University Press, 1990.

Nozari, Fariborz. *Unequal Treaties in International law*. Stockholm: S-Byran Sundt and Co., 1971.

Nussbaum, Arthur. *A Concise History of the Law of Nations*. New York: Macmillan, 1947.

Onuf, Nicholas. *World of Our Making: Rules and Rule in Social Theory and International Relations*. Columbia: University of South Carolina Press, 1989.

Onuf, Nicholas. "Constructivism: A User's Manual." In *International Relations in a Constructed World*. Edited by V. Kubalkova, N. Onuf, and P. Kowert, 58–78. Armonk, NY: M.E. Sharpe, 1998.

Oppenheim, Lassa. *International Law*. London: Longmans and Green, 1905.

Oppenheim, Lassa, ed. *Collected Papers of John Westlake*. Cambridge: Cambridge University Press, 1914.

Oros, Andrew L. *Normalizing Japan: Politics, Identity, and the Evolution of Security Practice*. Stanford, CA: Stanford University Press, 2008.

Panikkar, K. M. *Asia and Western Dominance: A Survey of the Vasco Da Gama Epoch of Asian History, 1498–1945*. London: George Allen and Unwin, 1953.

Perry, Commodore Matthew Calbraith. *The Japan Expedition, 1852–1854: The Presonal Journal of Commodore Matthew C. Perry*. Edited by Roger Pineau. Washington, D.C.: Smithsonian Institution Press, 1968.

Philpott, D. *Revolutions in Sovereignty: How Ideas Shaped Modern International Relations*. Princeton, NJ: Princeton University Press, 2001.

Piggott, Sir Francis. *Exterritoriality: The Law Relating to Consular Jurisdiction and to Residence in Oriental Countries*. London: Clowes, 1907.

Porter, Brian, ed. *The Aberystwth Papers*. Oxford: Oxford University Press, 1972.

Putnam, Robert D. *Making Democracy Work: Civic Traditions in Modern Italy*. Princeton, NJ: Princeton University Press, 1993.

Ram, K. V. "The Survival of Ethiopian Independence." *Conquest and Resistance to Colonialism in Africa*. Edited by Gregory Maddox. New York: Garland, 1993.

Resende-Santos, Joao. "Anarchy and the Emulation of Military Systems: Military Organization and Technology in South America, 1870–1930." *Security Studies* 5, no. 3 (1996): 193–260.

Riker, William H. "Implications from the Disequilibrium of Majority Rule for the Study of Institutions." *American Political Science Review* 74, no. 2 (1980): 444–45.

Risse, Thomas, and Kathryn Sikkink. "The Socialization of International Human Rights Norms into Domestic Practices; Introduction." In *The Power of Human Rights: International Norms and Domestic Change*. Edited by Thomas Risse and Kathryn Sikkink, 1–38. Cambridge: Cambridge University Press, 1999.

Roberts, Clayton. *The Logic of Historical Explanation*. University Park: Pennsylvania State University Press, 1996.

Rosovsky, Henry. *Capital Formation in Japan*. Glencoe: Free Press, 1961.

Röling, B.V.A. *International Law in an Expanded World*. Amsterdam: Djambatan, 1960.

Said, E. *Orientalism*. New York: Vintage, 1979.

Sansom, George B. *The Western World and Japan: A Study in the Interaction of Eastern and Asiatic Cultures*. London: The Cresset Press, 1965.

Satow, Ernest M. *A Diplomat in Japan*. Oxford: Oxford University Press, 1968.

Saussure, Fredinand de. *Course in General Linguistics*. Translated by Roy Harris. Chicago: Open Court Classics, 1972.

Schimmelfennig, Frank. "International Socialisation in the New Europe: Rational Action in an Institutional Environment." *European Journal of International Relations* 6, no. 1 (2000): 109–39.

Schroeder, Paul W. *The Transformation of European Politics 1763–1848*. Oxford: Clarendon, 1996.

Schwarzenberger, Georg. "The Standard of Civilisation in International Law." In *Current Legal Problems*. Edited by George W. Keeton and Georg Schwarzenberger. London: Stevens & Sons, 1955.

Schwarzenberger, Georg. *The Frontiers of International Law*. London: Stevens & Sons, 1962.

Schwarzenberger, Georg. *The Dynamics of Law*. Abingdon: Professional Books, 1976.

Schwarzenberger, Georg. *A Manual of International Law*. 6th ed. Abingdon: Professional Books, 1976.

Shelton, Dinah, ed. *Commitment and Compliance: The Role of Non-Binding Norms in the International Legal System*. Oxford: Oxford University Press, 2000.

Siebold, Alexander von. *Japan's Accession to the Comity of Nations*. London: Kegan Paul, 1901.

Sigel, R. "Assumptions about the Learning of Political Values." *Annals of the American Academy of Political and Social Science* 361 (1965): 1–9.

Silberman, Bernard S. *Cages of Reason: The Rise of the Rational State in France, Japan, the United States, and Great Britain*. Chicago: University of Chicago Press, 1992.

Simon, W. M. *European Positivism in the Nineteenth Century*. New York: Cornell University Press, 1966.

Slaughter, Anne-Marie, Andrew S. Tulumello, and Stepan Wood. "International Law and International Relations Theory: A New Generation of Interdisciplinary Scholarship." *American Journal of International Law* 92, no. 3 (1998): 367–97.

Slaughter, Anne-Marie. "International Law and International Relations Theory: A Dual Agenda." *American Journal of International Law* 87 (1993): 205–39.

Smith, Thomas C. *Political Change and Industrial Development in Japan: Government Enterprise, 1868–1880*. Stanford, CA: Stanford University Press, 1955.

Smith, Thomas C. "Japan's Aristocratic Revolution." *Yale Review* 50 (1961): 370–84.

Soothill, W. *China and the West*. London: Oxford University Press, 1925.

Sousa, N. *Capitulatory Regime of Turkey*. Baltimore: Johns Hopkins University Press, 1933.

Spruyt, Hendrik. *The Sovereign State and Its Competitors*. Princeton, NJ: Princeton University Press, 1994.

Spruyt, Hendrik. "Institutional Selection in International Relations: State Anarchy as Order." *International Organization* 48, no. 4 (1994): 527–57.

Steinmo, Sven, and Kathleen Thelen. "Historical Institutionalism in Comparative Politics." In *Structuring Politics: Historical Institutionalism in Comparative Analysis*. Edited by Sven Steinmo, Kathleen Thelen, and Frank Longstreth. Cambridge: Cambridge University Press, 1992.

Stern, John Peter. *The Japanese Interpretation of the "Law of Nations," 1854–1874*. Princeton, NJ: Princeton University Press, 1979.

Storry, Richard. *The Double Patriots*. London: Chatto and Windus, 1957.

Storry, Richard. *Japan and the Decline of the West in Asia, 1894–1943*. London: Macmillan, 1979.

Strang, David. "From Dependency to Sovereignty: An Event History Analysis of Decolonisation 1870–1987." *American Sociological Review* 55, no. 6 (1990): 846–60.

Stryker, S., and A. Statham. "Symbolic Interaction and Role Theory." In *The Handbook of Social Psychology* 1. Edited by G. Lindzey and E. Aronson, 31178. New York: Random House, 1985.

Suganami, Hidemi. "Japan's Entry into International Society." In *The Expansion of International Society*. Edited by Hedley Bull and Adam Watson. Oxford: Clarendon, 1984.

Sumiyoshi, Yoshihito. "State Practices and Interpretation of International Law in Early Japan (1865–)," *Meiji Law Journal* 2 (1995): 15–40.

Suzuki, Shogo. *Civilization and Empire: China and Japan's Encounter with European International Society*. New York: Routledge, 2009.

Takahashi, Sakuye. *Cases on International Law during the Chino-Japanese War*. Cambridge: Cambridge University Press, 1899.

Takahashi, Sakuye. *International Law Applied in the Russo-Japanese War with the Decisions of the Japanese Prize Courts*. London: Stevens and Sons, 1908.

Thelen, Kathleen. "Historical Institutionalism in Comparative Politics." *Annual Review of Political Science* 2, no. 1 (1999): 369–404.

Thies, Cameron G. "Sense and Sensibility in the Study of State Socialisation: A Reply to Kai Alderson." *Review of International Studies* 29, no. 4 (2003): 543–50.

Thies, Cameron G. "State Socialization and Structural Realism." *Security Studies* 19, no. 4 (2010): 689–717.

Thies, Cameron G. "International Socialization Processes vs. Israeli National Role Conceptions: Can Role Theory Integrate IR Theory and Foreign Policy Analysis?" *Foreign Policy Analysis* 8, no. 1 (2012): 25–46.

Thomas, George M., and John W. Meyer. "The Expansion of the State." *Annual Review of Sociology* 10, no. 1 (1984): 461–82.

Thomson, Janice E. "State Sovereignty in International Relations: Bridging the Gap between Theory and Empirical Research." *International Studies Quarterly* 39, no. 2 (1995): 213–33.

Thucydides. *History of the Peloponnesian War (Book 5:89).* London: Penguin Classics, 1972.

Tieya, Wang. "International Law in China: Historical and Contemporary Perspectives." Recueil de cours [collected courses]. Edited by Academie du droit international [Hague academy of international law]. Leiden: Martines Nijhoff Publishers, 1985: 232–37.

Tilly, Charles. "Reflections on the History of European State-Making." In *The Formation of National States in Western Europe*. Edited by Charles Tilly, 84–163. Princeton, NJ: Princeton University Press, 1975.

Tilly, Charles. "War-making and State-making as Organised Crime." In *Bringing the State Back In*. Edited by Peter Evans, Dietrich Rueschemeyer, and Theda Skocpol. Cambridge: Cambridge University Press, 1985.

Tilly, Charles. *Coercion, Capital, and European States, A.D. 990–1990*. Cambridge: Blackwell, 1990.

Toby, Ronald P. *State and Diplomacy in Early Modern Japan: Asia in the Development of the Tokugawa Bakufu*. Stanford, CA: Stanford University Press, 1984.

Toynbee, A. J. *A Study of History*. London: Oxford University Press, 1946.

Treat, Payson J. *The Diplomatic Relations between the United States and Japan, 1853–95*. Stanford, CA: Stanford University Press, 1932.

Trimberger, Ellen. *Revolution from Above: Military Bureaucrats and Development in Japan, Turkey, Egypt, and Peru*. New Brunswick, NJ: Transaction Books, 1978.

Turner, Sir Skinner. "Extraterritoriality in China." *British Yearbook of International Law*10 (1929): 56–64.

Twiss, Sir Travers, Q.C. *La jurisdiction consulaire dans les pays de l'orient et specialement au Japon*. Charlston: Biblio Life, 2010 (reprint).

Umesao, Tadao. "Japan as Viewed from an Eco-Historical Perspective." *Review of Japanese Culture and Society* 1, no 1 (1986): 25–31.

Umesao, Tadao. "Introduction to an Ecological View of Civilization." *Japan Echo* 22, Special Issue (1995): 42–50.

Umesao, Tadao. *An Ecological View of History: Japanese Civilization in the World Context*. International Specialized Book Service, 2003.

Veblen, Thorstein. "The Opportunity of Japan." *Journal of Race Development* 6, no. 1 (1915): 23–38.

Verzijl, J.H.W. "Western European Influence on the Foundations of International Law." In *International Law in Historical Perspective*. Leiden: Sijthoff, 1968: 435–6.

Von Martens, Georg Friedrich. *Precis du droit des gens moderne de l'Europe*. Paris: Guillaumin, 1858.

Wakabayashi, Bob Tadashi. *Anti-Foreignism and Western Learning in Early-Modern Japan: The New Theses of 1825*. Cambridge, MA: Harvard University Press, 1992.

Waltz, Kenneth N. *Man, the State, and War: A Theoretical Analysis*. New York: Columbia University Press, 1959.

Waltz, Kenneth N. *Theory of International Politics*. New York: McGraw-Hill, 1979.

Ward, Robert, and Dankwart Rustow. *Political Modernization in Japan and Turkey*. Princeton, NJ: Princeton University Press, 1964.

Ward, Robert, ed. *Political Development in Modern Japan*. Princeton, NJ: Princeton University Press, 1968.

Watson, Adam. *The Evolution of International Society: A Comparative Historical Analysis*. London: Routledge, 1992.

Wendt, Alexander E. "The Agent-Structure Problem in International Relations Theory." *International Organization* 41, no. 3 (1987): 335–70.

Wendt, Alexander E. "Collective Identity Formation and the International State." *American Political Science Review* 88, no. 2 (1994): 384–96.

Wendt, Alexander E. *Social Theory of International Politics*. Cambridge: Cambridge University Press, 1999.

Westlake, John. *Principles of International Law*. Cambridge: Cambridge University Press, 1894.

Westney, Eleanor. *Imitation and Innovation: The Transfer of Western Organizational Patterns to Meiji Japan*. Cambridge, MA: Harvard University Press, 1987.

Wheaton, Henry. *Elements of International Law*. Boston: Little Brown and Company, 1832.

Wight, Colin. *Agents, Structures and International Relations: Politics of Ontology*. New York: Cambridge University Press, 2006.

Wight, Martin. *International Theory: The Three Traditions*. London: Leicester Universtiy Press, 1991.

Wight, Martin. *Power Politics*. London: Leicester University Press, 1978.

Wight, Martin. *Systems of States*. London: Leicester University Press, 1977.

Williamson, Oliver. *Markets and Hierarchies*. New York: The Free Press, 1975.

Williamson, Oliver. *Economic Organization*. New York: New York University Press, 1986.

Young, Louis. *Japan's Total Empire: Manchuria and the Culture of Wartime Imperialism*. Berkeley: University of California Press, 1999.

Zhang, Yongjin. "China's Entry into International Society: Beyond the Standard of 'Civilisation'." *Review of International Studies* 17, no. 1 (1991): 3–16.

Zhang, Yongjin. *China in International Society since 1949*. New York: St. Martin's, 1998.

Sources in Japanese

Amino, Yoshihiko. *Nihon no Rekishi wo Yominaosu* [Rethinking of the Japanese History]. Tokyo: Chikuma Shobō, 1990.

Amino, Yoshihiko. *Zoku Nihon no Rekishi wo Yominaosu* [Rethinking of the Japanese History Ctnd.]. Tokyo: Chikuma Shobō, 1995.

Amino, Yoshihiko. *Nihon Shakai no Rekishi* [History of the Japanese Society]. Tokyo: Iwanami, 1997.

Ariga, Nagao. *Nisshin Sen'eki Kokusaihōron* [Sino-Japanese War in Light of International Law]. Tokyo: National Army Academy, 1896.

Banno, Masataka. *Kindai Chūgoku Seiji Gaikōshi* [Political and Diplomatic History of Modern China]. Tokyo: Tokyo University Press, 1973.

Bito, M. *Edo Jidai to wa Nanika* [What is Edo Period?]. Tokyo: Iwanami, 1992.

Dai Nihon Komonjo: Bakumatsu Gaikoku Kankei Monjo [Diplomatic Documents of Japan: Foreign Relations at the End of Edo]. Edited by Tokyo Teikoku Daigaku [Tokyo Imperial University]. Tokyo: Tokyo Daigaku Shiryō Hensansho [Center for Complilation of Historical Documents, University of Tokyo], 2005.

Fujita, Hisakazu. "Tōyō Shokoku eno Kokusaihō no Tekiyō: Jūkyū Seiki Kokusaihō no Seikaku [Application of International Law to Eastern Countries: Characteristics of the Nineteenth- Century International Law]." In *Hō to Seiji no Riron to Genjitsu* [Theory and Reality of Law and Politics] 1. Edited by Kansai University Law Faculty. Tokyo: Yūhikaku, 1979.

Fujita, Hisakazu. "Nihon ni okeru Sensōhō Kenkyū no Ayumi [History of Japanese Study on Law of War]." *Journal of Law and Diplomacy* 96 (1996): 600–12.

Fukuzawa, Yukichi. *Bunmeiron no Gairyaku* [An Outline of Theories of Civilization]. Tokyo: Iwanami Bunko, 1995. (Original work published 1875.)

Fukuzawa, Yukichi. *Fukuō Jiden* [The Autobiography of Fukuzawa Yukichi]. Tokyo: Iwanami Bunko, 2001.

Fukuzawa, Yukichi. *Fukuzawa Yukichi Chosakushū I: Seiyō Jijō* [Collected Works of Fukuzawa Yukichi I: Conditions in the West]. Tokyo: Keiō University Press, 2002. (Original work published 1866.)

Gaimushō. *Tsūshin Zenran* [Correspondence], 1–6. Tokyo: Yūshōdō Shoten, 1983.

Gaimushō. *Zoku Tsūshin Zenran* [Correspondence, ctnd.]. Tokyo: Yūshōdō Shoten, 1983.

Gaimushō Chōsabu. *Dai Nihon Gaikō Monjo* [Diplomatic Documents of Greater Japan]. Tokyo: Nihon Kokusai Kyōkai, 1911.

Gaimushō Chōsabu. *Nihon Gaikō Monjo* [Diplomatic Documents of Japan]. Digital Archive of the Documents on Japanese Foreign Policy. (www.mofa.go.jp/mofaj/annai/honsho/shiryo/archives/).

Gaimushō Gaikō Shiryōkan. *Nihon Gaikōshi Jiten* [Dictionary of Japanese Foreign Policy]. Tokyo: Nihon Gaikōshi Jiten Hensan Iinkai, 1992.

Hamashita, Takeshi. *Kindai Chūgoku no Kokusaiteki Keiki* [International Factors in Modern China]. Tokyo: University of Tokyo Press, 1990.

Hamashita, Takeshi. "Sōshuken no Rekishi Saikuru: Higashi Ajia Chiiki wo Chūshin toshite [Historical Cycle of Suzerainty in East Asia]." *Rekishigaku Kenkyū* [Study of History] 690 (1996): 2–11.

Harris, Townsend. *Nihon Taizaiki.* [The Complete Journal of Townsend Harris]. Translated by Seiichi Sakata. Tokyo: Iwanami Bunko, 1953.

Hayami, Akira, and M. Miyamoto, eds. *Nihon Keizai-shi.* [History of Japanese Economy]. Tokyo: Iwanami Shoten, 1988.

Higashi Ajia Kindaishi Gakkai [Association of Modern East Asian History]. *Higashi Ajia Kindaishi* [Modern History of East Asia] 2 (Special issue on "Adoptation and Adaptation of International Law in East Asia"). Tokyo: Yumani Shobō, 1999.

Higashi Ajia Kindaishi Gakkai [Association of Modern East Asian History]. *Higashi Ajia Kindaishi* [Modern History of East Asia] 3 (Special issue on "Modern International Law in Asia"). Tokyo: Yumani Shobō, 2000.

Hirose, Kazuko. "Kokusaishakai no Hendō to Kokusaihō no Ippanka [Change of International Society and Generalization of International Law]." In Ribō Hatano, Hajime Terasawa, Wakamizu Tsutsui, and Sōji Yamamoto, eds. *Kokusaihōgaku no Saikōchiku* [Reconstruction of the Study of International Law]. Tokyo: Tokyo University Press, 1978.

Hori, Toshikazu. *Chūgoku to Kodai Higashiajiasekai* [China and the Ancient East Asian World]. Tokyo: Iwanami, 1993.

Hosono, Kōji. "Seiyō no Shōgeki wo Meguru Nihon to Chūgoku no Taiyō [Japan and China in Countering the Western Impact] I." *Waseda Daigaku Daigakuin Bungaku Kenkyūka Kiyō* [Bulletin of the Graduate School of Literature at the University of Waseda] 36 (1990): 141–59.

Hosono, Kōji. "Seiyō no Shōgeki wo Meguru Nihon to Chūgoku no Taiyō [Japan and China in Countering the Western Impact] II." *Waseda Daigaku Daigakuin Bungaku Kenkyūka Kiyō* [Bulletin of the Graduate School of Literature at the University of Waseda] 37 (1991): 95–112.

Ichimata, Masao. "Meiji Oyobi Taishō Shoki ni okeru Nihon Kokusaihōgaku no Keisei to Hatten [Formation and Development of the Japanese International Legal Studies during the Meiji and Early Taishō]." *Journal of Law and Diplomacy* 70 (1972): 483–531.

Inō, Tentarō, and Azusa Ōyama. "Kindai Higashi Ajia ni okeru Fubyōdō Jōyaku Taisei no Seiritsu [Establishment of the Unequal Treaty System in Modern East Asia]." Literature Department of Chūō University. *Kiyō: Shigaku Ka* [Bulletin of the History Department] 28 (1983): 61–81.

Inō, Tentarō, and Azusa Ōyama. ""Higashi Ajia ni okeru Fubyōdō Jōyaku Taisei no Kaisei to Kaishō [Revision and Lifting of the Unequal Treaties in East Asia]." Literature Department of Chūō University." *Kiyō: Shigaku Ka* [Bulletin of the History Department] 30 (1985): 1–16.

Inō, Tentarō. *Higashi Ajia ni okeru Fubyōdō Jōyaku Taisei to Kindai Nihon* [The System of Unequal Treaties in East Asia and Modern Japan]. Tokyo: Iwata Shoin, 1995.

Inoue, Kiyoshi. *Jōyaku Kaisei* [Revision of Unequal Treaties]. Tokyo: Iwanami, 1955.

Inoue, Mitsusada, Kazuo Kasahara, and Kota Kodama, eds. *Shōsetsu Nihonshi* [Detailed Japanese History]. Tokyo: Yamakawa, 1993.

Irie, Takanori. *Taiheiyō Bunmei no Kōbō* [Rise and Fall of the Pacific Civilization]. Tokyo: PHP, 1997.

Ishii, Kanji. *Meiji Ishin no Kokusaiteki Kankyō* [International Environment of Meiji Restoration]. Tokyo: Yoshikawa Kōbunkan, 1966.

Ishii, Kanji. *Meiji Ishin to Gaiatsu* [Meiji Restoration and Foreign Pressure]. Tokyo: Yoshikawa Kōbunkan, 1993.

Ishii, Kanji. "Bakumatsu Kaikō to Gaiatsu eno Taiō [Opening of Japan at the End of Edo and Japan's Response to Foreign Pressure]." In Nihon Keizai-shi [*Economic History of Japan*]. Edited by Akira Hara, Kanji Ishii, and Haruhito Takeda, vol. 1. Tokyo: Tokyo University Press, 2000.

Kagotani, Naoto. "1880 nendai no Ajia karano Shōgeki to Nihon no Hannō [Impact from Asia in 1880's and Japan's Response]." *Rekishigaku Kenkyū* [Study of History] 608 (1990): 1–18.

Kagotani, Naoto. "Ajia karano 'Shōgeki' to Nihon no Kindai [The 'Impact' from Asia and the Modernity of Japan]." *Nihon Shi Kenkyu* [Study of Japanese History] 344 (1991): 126–62.

Kasuya, Susumu. "Nihon no Kaikoku to Kokusaihō [Opening of Japan and International Law]." *Keizai Shūshi* [Papers on Economic History] 44 (1974): 648–58.

Katsu, Kaishū. *Hikawa Seiwa* [Collected Essays of Katsu Kaishū]. Edited by Jun Etō and Rei Matsuura. Tokyo: Kōdansha Gakujutsu Bunko, 2004.

Katsuyō, Jiten Henshu Iinkai. *Kuzushi ji Jiten* [Dictionary of Running Style of Japanese]. Tokyo: Kashiwa Shobō, 1982.

Kawakatsu, Heita. *Bunmei no Kaiyōshikan* [Maritime View of Civilization]. Tokyo: Chūō Kōronsha, 1997.

Kawashima, Shintarō. *Jōyaku Kaisei Keika Gaiyō* [An Overview of the Process of Revising the Unequal Treaties]. Tokyo: The United Nations Associations of Japan, 1950.

Kobayashi, Takashi. *Umi no Ajiashi* [Asian History from the Perspective of Sea]. Tokyo: Fujiwara Shoten, 1997.

Kōzai, Shigeru. "Bakumatsu Kaikokuki ni okeru Kokusaihō no Dōnyū [Introduction of International Law in the Opening of Japan at the End of Edo Period]." *Hōgaku Ronsō* [Debates on Legal Studies] 97 (1975): 1–38.

Kōzai, Shigeru. "Japan's Early Practice of International Law: The Law of Neutrality." *International Studies* (The International Studies Association of Ōsaka Gakuin University) 7, no. 1 (1996): 1–26.

Kume, Kunitake, ed. *Tokumei Zenken Taishi Beiō Kairan Jikki* [Chronicle of the Mission of the Special Ambassadors Plenipotentiary to America and Europe]. 5 vols. Tokyo: Iwanami Bunko, 1977.

Lee, Kwang-rin. "The Introduction of the 'Wan-kuo kung-fa' to Korea'." East Asian Studies. *The Journal of the Institute for East Asian Studies, Sogan University* (December, 1982): 121–45.

Maruyama, Masao. "Fukuzawa Yukichi no Tetsugaku [Philosophy of Fukuzawa Yukichi]." *Kokka Gakkai Zasshi* [Journal of Association of States] 61, no. 3 (1947): 129–63.

Maruyama, Masao. *Bunmeiron no Gairyaku wo Yomu* [Reading Fukuzawa's "Bunmeiron no Gairyaku"]. Tokyo: Iwanami Shinsho, 1986.

Makoto, Kawashima. *Chūgoku Kindai Gaikō no Keisei* [Formation of the Chinese Modern Diplomacy]. Nagoya: Nagoya University Press, 2004.

Mori, Seiichi. "Paterunosutoro to Jōyaku Kaisei [Paternostro and Revision of Unequal Treaties]." *Hōgaku Kenkyū* [Study of Law] 69 (1996): 43–64.

Moriya, Hidesuke. *Jōyaku Kaisei* [Revision of Unequal Treaties]. Tokyo: Iwanami Shoten, 1934.

Motegi, Toshio. *Hen'yō surù Kindai Higashiajia no Kokusai Chitsujo* [International Order of Transforming Modern East Asia]. Tokyo: Yamakawa, 1997.

Murase, Shinya. "Nihon no Kokusaihōgaku ni okeru Hōgenron no Isō [The Sources of Law in the Japanese Study of International Law]." *Journal of Law and Diplomacy* 96, no. 45 (1996): 723–51.

Mutsu, Munemitsu. *Kenken Roku* [My Uphill Struggle]. Tokyo: Iwanami Bunko, 1983. (Original work published 1895.)

Nihon no Rekishi. Asahi Newspaper Company. 50 vols.

Ōhira, Zengo. "Nihon no Kokusaihō no Juyō [Japan's Acceptance of International Law]." *Shōgaku Tōkyū* [Discussions on Commerce] 4 (1953): 299–314.

Okamoto, Takashi. "Kaikō to Chōkō no Aida: Gokō Kaikō Jidai no Fuzhou wo Chūshin ni [Between the Opening of the Treaty Ports and the Tributary Trade on the China Coast With Special Reference to Fuzhou. 1844-1859]." *Miyazaki Daigaku Kyōiku Gakubu Kiyō, Shakai Kagaku* [Bulletin of the Educational Department of the University of Miyazaki, Social Science] 81 (1996): 1–24.

Ōkubo, Toshiaki. *Kindaishi Shiryō* [Documents of Modern Japanese History]. Tokyo: Yoshikawa, 1965.

Osatake, Takeki. "Bakumatsu ni okeru Kokusaihō [International Law at the End of Edo Bakufu]." Hōgaku Shirin [Study of Law] 16, no. 6 (1914): 15–34.

Osatake, Takeki. *Kokusaihō yori Mitaru Bakumatsu Gaikō Monogatari* [Diplomatic Story at the End of Edo from the Perspective of International Law]. Tokyo: Bunka Seikatsu Kenkyūkai, 1926.

Ozawa, Ichiro. "Futsuno no Kuni ni Nare [Become a Normal Country]." In *Sengo Nihon Gaikō Ronshū* [Postwar Japanese Diplomatic Writings]. Edited by Shin'ichi Kitaoka. Tokyo: Chūō Kōron Sha, 1995.

Sasaki, Yō. "Shindai no Chōkō Sisutemu to Kingendai Chūgoku no Sekaikan [The Ch'ing Tribute System and Modern China's View of the World]." *Saga Daigaku Kyōikugakubu Ronbunshū* [Collection of essays of the Educational Department of the University of Saga] 34, no. 2: 74–46; 35, no. 2: 128–11 (1987 and 1988).

Satō, Seizaburō. *Shi no Chōyaku: Seiyō no Shōgeki to Nihon* [Deathly Leap: The Western Impact and Japan]. Tokyo: Toshi Shuppan, 1992.

Satow, Ernest. *Ichi Gaikōkan no Mita Meiji Ishin* [The Meiji Restoration Seen by a Diplomat]. Translated by Seiichi Sakata. Tokyo: Iwanami Bunko, 1960.

Seki, Shizuo, ed. *Kindai Nihon Gaikō Shisōshi Nyūmon* [Introduction to the Diplomatic Thoughts in Modern Japan]. Tokyo: Minerva, 1999.

Shinobu, Junpei. "Vicissitudes of International Law in the Modern History of Japan." *Journal of Law and Diplomacy* 50, no. 2 (May, 1951): 196–234.

Shinoda, Harusaku. *Nichiro Sen'eki Kokusaikōhō* [Russo-Japanese War in Light of International Public Law]. Tokyo: Hōsei University Press, 1911.

Shumitto, Kāru. *Daichi no Nomosu* [Karl Schmit, Der Nomos der Erde im Völkerrecht des Jus Publicum Europaeum]. Translated by Kunio Nitta. Tokyo: Fukumura, 1984.

Sumiyoshi, Yoshihito. "Seiō Kokusai Hōgaku no Nihon eno Inyū to Sono Tenkai [Introduction of the Western International Law to Japan and Its Development]." *Hōritsu Ronsō* [Debates on Law] 42 (1969): 343–70.

Sumiyoshi, Yoshihito. "Meiji Shoki ni okeru Kokusaihō no Dōnyū [Introduction of International Law in the Early Meiji]." *Journal of Law and Diplomacy* 70 (1972): 454–79.

Tabata, Shigejirō. "Ajia Afurika Shinkō Shokoku to Kokusaihō [Asian and African States and International Law]." *Shisō* [Social Thought] 496 (1965): 9–17.

Tada, Komon, ed. *Iwakura Ko Jikki* [A True Record of Prince Iwakura]. Tokyo: Hara Shobo, 1968.

Takahashi, Sakue. *Kokusaihō Gaikō Ronsan* [Studies in International Law and Diplomacy]. Tokyo: Shimizu Shoten, 1903–1904.

Takahashi, Sakue . "Meiji Jidai ni okeru Kokusaihō Kenkyū no Hattatsu [Development of International Law during the Meiji Era]." Hōgaku Kyōkai Zasshi [Journal of the Jurisprudence Association] 30, no. 12 (1912): 46–64.

Takahashi, Sakue, and Nakamura Shingo. *Senji Kokusai Kōhō* [International Law of War]. Tokyo: Nihon University Press, n.d.

Takahashi, Sakue, and Endō Genroku. *Senji Kokusaihō Kōgi* [Lecture on International Law of War]. Tokyo: Meiji University Press, n.d.

Taoka, Ryōichi. "Nishi Shūsuke 'Bankoku Kōhō' [Nishi Shūsuke's International law]." *Journal of Law and Diplomacy* 70 (1972): 1–57.

Toriumi, Yasushi, Masato Matsuo, and Hideo Kokaze. *Nihon Kingendaishi Kenkyū Jiten* [Encyclopedia of Modern and Contemporary Japanese History]. Tokyo: Tokyōdō Shuppan, 1999.

Tsuishōkai, Shunpokō. *Itō Hitobumi Den* [Biography of Itō Hirobumi]. Tokyo: Tōseisha, 1940.

Tsutsui, Wakamizu. "Hi Yōroppa Chiiki to Kokusaihō [Non-European Regions and International Law]." *Seijikeizaironsō* [Debates on Political Economy]. (January 1965): 59–80.

Tsutsui, Wakamizu. *Sensō to Hō* [War and Law]. Tokyo: Tokyo University Press, 1971.

Umesao, Tadao. *Bunmei no Seitaishi Kan* [An Ecological View of History]. Tokyo: Chūō Kōron Sha, 1967.

Yamamoto, Shigeru. *Jōyaku Kaiseishi* [History of Revising Unequal Treaties]. Tokyo: Takayama Shoin, 1943.

Yamamuro, Shin'ichi. *Shisō Kadai toshite no Ajia* [Asia as a Theme of Thoughts]. Tokyo: Iwanami, 2001.

Yasuoka, Akio. "Bankoku Kōhō to Meiji Gaikō [International Law and Meiji Diplomacy]." *Seiji Keizaishi Gaku* [Studies on the History of Political Economy] 200 (1983): 188–99.

Acknowledgments

My gratitude is inexhaustible in acknowledging all the help and support that I have received over the years during the long process of producing this book. The project started with the guidance of my former doctoral advisor at the University of Michigan, Harold Jacobson, who passed away in August 2001, on the very day I went back to Japan to conduct my research after a two-year stay in Ann Arbor supported by a Fulbright scholarship. Despite the great sense of loss that his passing left with me, I am deeply appreciative of his encouragement, trust, and confidence in this project at the initial stage of writing a draft. I am endlessly grateful to John Campbell, who took over as the committee chair with his exceptional talent for getting to the essence of the matter brilliantly, whether in critiquing the manuscript or in advising on technicalities. The first manuscript of the book would not have been completed without his help and direction. Whenever I am in contact with him, he still continues to inspire me and reminds me of what constitutes a good academic.

Most of the revising of the manuscript was conducted while I was an academic associate at the Program on US-Japan Relations at the Weatherhead Center (2007–8) and a visiting scholar at the Reischauer Institute of Japanese Studies (2009–10), both at Harvard University. I benefited immensely from the warm, congenial environment full of lively academic spirits, conversations with my colleagues, and the excellent library resources of Yenching, Gutman, Widener, and Fung, in particular. An Abe fellowship generously gave me financial support for these two stays at Harvard. My debts are exceptionally heavy in nature in receiving not only academic but also administrative support from Fujihira Shinju, Ted Gilman, Montana Higo, Lianna Kushi, Stacie Matsumoto,

William Nehring, Sakaguchi Kazuko, and Susan Wagner. At the last stage of writing this manuscript, the Faculty of Law at Dokkyo University provided with me an agreeable working environment. I thank my colleague professors and students from the bottom of my heart.

I would like to further extend my heartfelt gratitude to those who have helped me during the process of writing and revising the manuscript over the years with their professional advice. Many of them read a portion of the earlier draft: Albert Craig, Gerrit Gong, Andrew Gordon, Peter Hall, Douglas Howland, Robert Jackson, Alastair Johnston, Charles Maier, Lisa Martin, Robert Paarlberg, Susan Pharr, Beth Simmons, Tonomura Hitomi, the late Kenneth Waltz, David Welch, and William Zimmerman. A short version of this work appeared in the form of a Japanese article in *Kokuksai Seiji* (International Relations) in 2003, on which Ishida Atsushi kindly shared his insights in improving my ideas. Previously I had also learned greatly from the conferences and workshops that I participated in at The Hague (2004) and Monterey (2003), where I received invaluable comments and suggestions for my presentations on the theme of this book.

Working on this book has been a humbling yet enriching experience. I am grateful to the University of Toronto Press for giving me such an excellent opportunity to present my idea to the public. I have especially appreciated the efficient management and encouragement of Daniel Quinlan of the press that always lifted my spirits in the process of writing. My thanks further go to the book committee members, including the three anonymous reviewers, who provided me with insightful pieces of advice for refining the manuscript.

At the completion of the book, I feel most appreciative of those who have consistently given me moral support in the forms of friendship, soul-mateship, child-support, emergency shelter, pick-me-up-food provision, and in many other displays of kindness and generosity over the years. My special thanks to Atake Masako, Beppu Yuriko and the late Beppu Tetsuo, Jim Blum, Ethel and Bill Braverman, Chizuko Muranaka Broinowski, Megan Brown, Steven Fabian, Hanashima Tomoko, Kyle Hecht, Okyeon Yi Hong, Su-Feng Kuo, Fabio Marchesoni, Petula Muller and the late George Kresina, Mark Norman, Okada Miki, Okagaki Keiko and Takayuki, Sato Itaru, Sun Tao, Christof Weil, Xiujuan Zhang and an endless list of capable multinational babysitters and housekeepers who assisted me in Ann Arbor, Cambridge, and Tokyo.

I dedicate this book with humility to my children, Alyssa, Leo, and Ray (alphabetical), in appreciation for the high morale that they have managed to maintain in support of me in different shades and gradations of my life. The book is in many ways a belated receipt for their unfailing cheer, for which I have been most grateful.

Index

Japan and Global Society

Japan as a 'Normal Country'? A Nation in Search of Its Place in the World, edited byYoshihide Soeya, Masayuki Tadokoro, and David A. Welch

The Evolution of Japan's Party System: Politics and Policy in an Era of Institutional Change, edited by Leonard J. Schoppa

Tumultuous Decade: Empire, Society, and Diplomacy in 1930s Japan, edited by Masato Kimura and Tosh Minohara

The Logic of Conformity: Japan's Entry into International Society, by Tomoko T. Okagaki

www.ingramcontent.com/pod-product-compliance
Lightning Source LLC
LaVergne TN
LVHW090159080826
844660LV00013B/877/J
9781442641884